CONVENTION

By Richard Reeves

A Ford, not a Lincoln
Old Faces of 1976
Convention

Photographs by Elliott Erwitt

Richard ☒
Reeves _____

Additional reporting for
this book was done by: Barry M. Hager   Peter W

CONVENTION

aplan   Brooke Shearer   Amanda Urban   Jean Vallely   Edward P. Whelan

HARCOURT BRACE JOVANOVICH   NEW YORK AND LONDON

This book is for Tony Godwin

⊠ Contents

"There are ten thousand campaigns going on at this convention, and Jimmy Carter's is only one of them."

—*Greg Schneiders, aide to Jimmy Carter*

☒ Preface

At one time or another, every young reporter runs into an old-timer who tells him that you can knock on any door and get a story. There were 25,000 doors at the 1976 Democratic Convention in New York City and we knocked on a lot of them. "We" were nine people who began covering the preparations for the event late in 1975, more than eight months before the opening gavel on July 12, 1976. In those months, we contacted several hundred men and women who expected to be in New York for that week in July—some of them never made it—and more than 50 agreed to keep written or taped journals of their four days in and around Madison Square Garden. We stopped counting the total number of interviews when it reached 500— that was two months before the Convention began.

The seven people who worked their way through Democratic National Committee meetings, precinct caucuses around the country, television network planning sessions, and everything from New York Police Department briefings to early morning discussions between pimps and prostitutes about whether politicians were good for business, were:

Barry Hager, Peter Kaplan, Brooke Shearer, Amanda Urban, Jean Vallely, Edward Whelan, and myself. We were joined at the convention by Richard Socarides and Nick Stadlan. In addition, more than 30 reporters covering the event volunteered to provide information for this book.

The idea for *Convention* came from Tony Godwin of Harcourt Brace Jovanovich. After Tony's death, Dan Okrent guided the project to completion. I received timely help from four friends: Ken Auletta, Jane O'Reilly, Steve Weisman, and Lynn Nesbit, my agent. Also helpful were Susan Parker, Judith Sandoval, and Merry Clark, all of *New York* magazine; Jean Kidd; and Roy McGhee and Louise Crow of the Senate Periodical Gallery. Marguerite Michaels and my children, Cindie and Jeff, put up with me, which was no small thing.

Most of all, I am in debt to the hundreds of delegates and others who cooperated in the making of this book, and I only wish that my gratitude always showed in the published word. The curse of writing is that, in the end, there is just you and the typewriter—admiration, affection, and laughs do not necessarily translate into kind words.

RICHARD REEVES
November 8, 1976

⊠ Prologue:
New York City 1976

Clare Smith arrived at New York City's John F. Kennedy International Airport at 6:40 on Sunday morning, July 11. She had gotten out of bed at 3:50 A.M. to make American Airlines Flight 38 from Cleveland at 5:20 A.M., saving $40 by flying night coach rate.

"Hey, excuse me," a young man called to her in the terminal. "Aren't you the youngest delegate to the Convention? I saw your picture in *People* magazine."

"Yeah."

"What hotel are you staying at? What's your name? What gate are you coming in at Madison Square Garden?"

"I was sort of flattered," she wrote that night in her diary. "But this guy was a real loser. Skinny, pimples, the whole bit."

Clare, though, was a winner. There were seven messages waiting for her when she arrived at the New York Sheraton Hotel after a $17 cab ride. Paula Slimak from Channel 5 in Cleveland found her in an elevator and persuaded her to repack her suitcases so that a crew could film her unpacking for the folks back home.

Seven reporters and four photographers surrounded the youngest delegate an hour later in the Sheraton lobby. "Look this way doll . . ." "C'mon, smile honey!" In her diary, Clare wrote, "Oh, screw you! . . . I soon learned that reporters attract other reporters; eventually you sound like a babbling seventeen-year-old idiot."

"John Glenn! John Glenn!" someone shouted, and Clare was abandoned. But only for a moment. Ohio's Lieutenant Governor Richard Celeste grabbed her—"Lord, I was getting a little sick of people grabbing me"—and rushed her over to shake hands with Senator Glenn, with Celeste smiling between them for the four photographers.

Jimmy Carter had come to town the day before, landing in his chartered Boeing 727 at the isolated Marine Air Terminal on the far side of La Guardia Airport. It was 3:30 in the afternoon, and he was early, as usual. After walking down the ramp carrying his own suitcase, as usual, and waving to television cameras, Carter was led into an empty operations office to kill ten minutes so that he would not arrive too early at a 4:00 P.M. rally in front of the Americana Hotel. In the office, Carter took off his shirt, and Secret Service agents helped him into a bulletproof vest for the rally. It was the first time the candidate had ever worn one, but the Secret Service had convinced him that he was beginning the most dangerous week of his political life.

There were 4,000 people waiting for Carter around the entrance of the Americana, a shiny 50-story piece of Miami Beach plunked down on Seventh Avenue in Manhattan, between 51st and 52nd Streets. "Inside the hotel, a technician named Richard Wilker was crawling through the candidate's suite, using a small mirror to check under doors for electronic listening devices—Carter's staff was convinced that reporters would try to bug his rooms."

He was certain to be the presidential nominee of the Democratic party, and now he wanted to have some fun about the guessing over his running mate: "I would like to announce my own personal choice for vice-president"— excited "oohs" came from the street—"as soon as I'm sure who the choice for president is going to be."

In the crowd, George Jordan, a retired Secret Service agent who had driven from his Long Island home, reminded his wife and children again that he knew Carter, that he had guarded the candidate during 1975 trips to Elmira and Brooklyn. When Carter walked up the Americana steps, waving, Jordan stepped toward him with a camera in his left hand and his right hand reaching out. "Mr. Carter, Mr. Carter," he said, almost touching the candidate before a young Secret Serviceman dropped his shoulder into Jordan, moving the old agent away from Carter.

Azie Morton, the deputy manager of the Convention, had moved from Washington to New York on October 18, 1975, to set up the Democratic National Committee's on-site office in the Madison Square Garden complex. On her first full day there, she tried to take the subway to City Hall and ended up in Brooklyn. "I consider myself a fairly intelligent human being," she told her boss, Democratic National Chairman Robert Strauss, "but no one from out of town can figure those trains out, even if they don't mind being pushed and shoved around. There's no way we're going to get delegates into that hole in the ground."

When the light above her desk blew out, she called the Garden's electrician. Two men arrived carrying a ladder, one to hold it and one to change the bulb. "How much is this going to cost?" she asked. Forty dollars.

She needed an electrical socket moved to plug in a Xerox machine, but this time when she called the Garden people, she asked the price first. Two hundred seventy dollars.

Thank you, she said, and reached for the Manhattan Yellow Pages. The first electrician she called said he could do the job for $70, but that he would have to charge the same $270 and pay the difference to the Garden's union to get into the building.

"This is insane," Mrs. Morton said. "This whole place is insane."

Hurley Goodall, a fireman from Muncie, Indiana, drove into New York on Sunday. He and his wife, Fredine, were registered at the Waldorf Astoria, but they went first to Carter headquarters at the Americana, where they were handed a check for $200 by a Carter staff member, Barbara Brenizer.

It was hush money, or an offering of conscience, depending on your perspective. No one, least of all Jimmy Carter, wanted Hurley Goodall to be unhappy, to start talking about how he had finally gotten to New York. He had worked three months for Carter back home, where he was a precinct committeeman in Delaware County, and delivered his precinct for the Georgian by a vote of 10-to-1 in Indiana's May 4 primary election, at the same time getting himself elected a delegate to the state Democratic convention. At the state convention in Indianapolis he was elected a national delegate, easily running first among 12 candidates from his congressional district. Then Carter's managers in Atlanta made a deal with the Indiana Labor Coalition, a powerful local alliance of eight national unions, giving the ILC 60 percent of Indiana's delegate seats in return for national union support in later primaries. Goodall and 23 other elected delegates and alternates were kicked out—under complicated Democratic National Committee (DNC) rules, presidential candidates had the power to certify or disqualify their own delegates. "I'm sorry, Hurley, you're out," said State Chairman William Trisler. "You're on your own."

On their own, Hurley and Fredine Goodall took off for Washington, D.C., in their 1972 Chevrolet pickup truck. They drove the 600 miles overnight on June 27, stopping to sleep for two hours in a closed gas station, to protest to the DNC's Credentials Committee. "I have been a member of the Democratic party since I cast my first ballot for Harry Truman," Goodall said, "stuffing envelopes, registering voters, passing out campaign literature, and getting out the vote on election days for over twenty-five years . . . I was duly elected . . . I appeal to you."

"You have won the hearts of the committee," said the chairman, Senator Alan Cranston of California. But not the votes—Goodall lost. The rules had been designed to stop delegates from declaring for one candidate during a primary and voting for another at a convention, but they were the rules no matter how cynically they had been used —and the committee upheld them.

Being black had not always been the best thing in Hurley Goodall's life—he was almost kept out of the Muncie Fire Department in 1958 to prevent "inevitable intermarriage of the races"—but this time it helped. Black members of the Credentials Committee threatened to file a minority report—there would be a floor fight in New York, a publicized floor fight over the screwing of Hurley Goodall. Within 20 minutes, Carter headquarters in Atlanta found a way to make Goodall an alternate to the Convention and said they would give him $200 to cover the expenses of his night-long drive to Washington.

Floor fights! Robert Schwarz Strauss had dedicated three and a half years of his life to figuring out how the Democratic party could meet in unified convention, quiet convention. He had become Democratic national chairman on December 9, 1972, determined that, while he was in charge, his party would not meet in riot, as it did in Chicago, nominating Hubert H. Humphrey for president in 1968, or in fiasco, as it did in Miami, nominating George McGovern in 1972. "I'm not going to deliver a candidate to the party," he said that December. "I'm going to deliver a party to the candidate."

Strauss arrived in New York on June 28, moving into a corner office on the second floor of the Statler Hilton Hotel across Seventh Avenue from Madison Square Garden, the site of the Thirty-seventh Convention of the Democratic Party of the United States. "Medicine depends on what ails you," he told a friend. "And I know what ails us and what medicine we need. We need a sedative." If he had his way, the Democrats would be sedated—and Bob Strauss would scream, bully, bluff, charm, crawl, and lie a bit to make sure of it.

One of Strauss's calls that first day was to John DeLury, the president of the Uniformed Sanitationmen's Association, the union representing the 10,000 men who clean the city's streets. The crew of out-of-towners delegated to run his Convention by Strauss, a Texan, had figured out after nine months that DeLury, not Mayor Beame or his commissioners, was the man who decided whether 25,000 delegates, alternates, reporters, and assorted guests and dignitaries would see midtown Manhattan as it usually is or would go back home saying it was cleaner than they had heard.

"Hello, John," said Strauss, who had never met DeLury. "I just wanted to call to gossip with you a bit about politics. About how we can elect ourselves a president of the United States.

"I want you to know that if there's anything I can ever do for you . . . I don't want to be presumptuous—but if you ever need any help, in Washington or anyplace . . .

"Everyone says New York is a dirty, filthy city . . . I

know, I know . . . I tell them that's not true, that you have the same problems as everyone else, just more intense. I want to know whether there's anything I can do for you to see that that thirty-square-block area around Madison Square Garden . . . that they see the cleanest this city can be.

"Okay, John. And after this convention there are some political things I want to talk to you about. And, John, if there's anything you need from me, tickets for the Convention, passes . . ."

On Sunday, the day before the Convention's first session, Strauss's offices were a cacophony of the pleas and cries of some of the most powerful men and women in the country, all wanting some of those tickets. The chairman tried to stay above most of it, but succeeded only in moving around it, running out of the office of one of his assistants, calling in three directions, "I'm sorry, Congressman . . ." "Tell the governor . . ." "I'll try, I'll try . . ." There was a call from the office of Representative Edward Boland saying that he wanted the passes of Torbert Macdonald, another Massachusetts congressman who had died on May 21, that one of Macdonald's last wishes was that Boland get his convention credentials. It was the second call that day from someone claiming Macdonald's final patronage.

But when Robert Walters, a writer for *Parade* magazine, came in and said the popular Sunday supplement was considering a cover story on Strauss, he was immediately handed three "Honored Guest" credentials for each night of the Convention, plus passes for the guarded lounge reserved for VIPs.

Representative Morris Udall of Arizona was applauded warmly, sometimes tearfully, as he appeared at his last rally before 1,000 people at the Roosevelt Hotel on East

45th Street near Grand Central Station. He reminded his faithful, including most of the 330 or so delegates he had won in primary elections and precinct caucuses, that he had been an announced candidate for president for 20 months, traveling to every part of the country, entering 22 primaries—and losing every one of them.

"The people have spoken—the bastards!"

It was an old line but a good one, and the audience laughed appreciatively, as Udall's crowd's often did—he was a nice man, for a politician, and his image had been softened by nine heartbreaking second-place finishes to Jimmy Carter. The man who had first used the line was in the crowd, wearing a floppy Panama hat and a grin wider and warmer than Carter's—Dick Tuck had defined the electorate as bastards 20 years earlier after losing a State Senate race in Los Angeles, and he had supported himself since as a political consultant/prankster. In fact, no one was quite sure of his means of support as he shuttled between New York and Aspen, Colorado, and any campaign that would have him. But at conventions, he did it by publishing a scurrilous and often funny little newspaper called *The Reliable Source,* which would then go out of business for four more years.

What the people had said in the 31 Democratic primaries was that they were annoyed, perhaps deeply angry, with Washington, that their capital seemed to have lost touch with reality and with their lives. They said it by voting again and again for Jimmy Carter, an almost unknown former governor of Georgia, and, later, for Jerry Brown, the deliberately enigmatic young governor of California.

Carter almost literally came from nowhere. At the 1972 convention, a California delegate cast a vote for him for vice-president, and Dorothy Bush, the secretary of the DNC for 32 years, had asked the delegate from the podium: "Governor *who?*" In 1973, he had appeared on the tele-

vision show "What's My Line?" and, even after being told
he was governor of Georgia, the celebrity panelists could
not guess his name. Less than a year before the Convention,
already a declared candidate for the presidency, Carter
had called a press conference in Philadelphia, and no one
came.

At 9:30 A.M. on Sunday the New York Fire Department received a first alarm from the Statler Hilton on
Seventh Avenue between 32nd and 33rd Streets, the headquarters hotel for the Convention. There was a lot of tired
wiring in the 57-year-old hotel, and some of it had short-
circuited, starting a small fire in the second-floor offices of
the Democratic National Committee, setting off the alarm
and a sprinkler system that left water dripping down elevator shafts.

"What a way to start," moaned Xavier Lividini, the
manager of what had been until 1927 the world's largest
hotel. "If I were a superstitious man . . ."

He was a nervous man who had replaced the ceramic
elephant in his office, a gift of a friend, with a bust of
John F. Kennedy—hiding the elephant in his closet because he was afraid the symbol of the Republican party
would offend Bob Strauss. "You and I are going to put
on a convention and nominate a president of the United
States," Strauss had said to him early in the year, playfully
pulling the hotelman toward him by the lapels of his tailored
Italian suit. "You won't choke on me, will you, Sal?"

Choking wasn't Lividini's style. He had worked his way
up from room clerk in this hotel, taking management jobs
around the country in the Statler chain and then the Hilton
chain after Conrad Hilton bought the Statler in 1954 and
added his name to it. Scurrying was Lividini's style—all
during the year of negotiations heading up to the Convention he had run back and forth in front of the hotel to

chase away prostitutes when important Democrats were coming in to talk. "Get away. Get away from here!" he yelled, waving his hands outward. His employees—the hotel had 800—and the $20 whores usually enjoyed it. He was a very small, fastidious man who liked to brag that he was taller than Mayor Abraham Beame, who was an inch or so above five feet.

Lividini and Beame had a lot in common. They were both running tired institutions, both afraid that time and technology were passing them by. The Statler, which was first called the Pennsylvania Hotel, had been built to serve the railroad travelers using Pennsylvania Station. But trains had been passed by planes; the station, which was now underground, beneath the Garden, was used mostly by commuters; and the stylish stores, Saks and Bonwit's, were now uptown. Even Bob Strauss was uptown, living at the Waldorf Astoria until the Convention actually began—and that was after Barron Hilton, Conrad's son, had authorized Lividini to go ahead with $4 million in renovations for the showcase event. More than a million dollars of that was just to replace the original cord-and-plug switchboard with a modern telephone system. The phone number stayed the same: Pennsylvania 6-5000, same as the Glenn Miller tune —the bandleader had met his wife there when the hotel, and the city, were a little classier.

Assistant Chief Daniel Courtenay, the commander of New York Police assigned to the Convention, had warned Democratic Convention officials about two things—bombs, and 5,000 to 10,000 out-of-town prostitutes expected in the city that week. Most of the prostitutes would probably be "Minnesotas," the New York cops' jargon for white professionals. "There are two things I want," Courtenay had told the 1,500 officers under him on Convention duty. "I don't want a delegate propositioned fifteen times on his way from the hotel to the Garden, and I don't want him propositioned anywhere while he's with his wife, okay? These people know this isn't Omaha, and they wouldn't be here if they didn't want a little action. But we're going to move the girls away a little, okay? Talk nice to them, they'll understand it's important."

New York vice cops almost always talked nice to "prosses." It was like any other business; people get to know each other, and they learn to get along. Anyway, the cops needed the girls to get what they really wanted, the pimps—"Macks," the big guys riding in customized Cadillacs, and "Popcorns" or "Macaronis," small-timers living off a junkie whore or two. In April, the New York Police Department had established a Pimp Squad, which was giving a special telephone number to prostitutes who wanted to turn in their male protectors and masters. On the Sunday before the Convention began, at 12:01 A.M., a new anti-loitering law had gone into effect, allowing an officer to arrest anyone he saw "beckon, stop, or engage passersby in conversation" for what the cop thought might be solicitation. There were doubts about the new ordinance's constitutionality, but appeals by the New York Civil Liberties Union would not be heard until after the Convention—and vice cops called it "the Convention law."

"I don't know what's going on or where the orders are coming from, but I think a lot of the girls would be smart to take a vacation this week," Lieutenant James Gallagher, head of the Public Morals Squad, told his men at their pre-Convention meeting. And, for the week, he had 48 extra men. In the previous two weeks the cops had arrested 400 prostitutes, compared with the usual 25 a week, and on Friday, city judges began sentencing hookers to 30 to 90 days in jail—in other weeks, they would be back on the streets within an hour of an arrest and small fine.

Before hitting the streets in two waves at 6 P.M. and

8:00 P.M.—concentrating on the city's three busiest "action" hotels, the Statler Hilton, the New York Hilton, and the Americana—the cops in the Morals Squad talked about putting up ten dollars each for their own "VIP Pool." The money would go to the man who caught a congressman with his pants down.

The Democrats Abroad delegation, representing the Democrats among more than 1 million Americans living outside the country, held their first caucus at ten o'clock Sunday morning in the Vanderbilt Suite of the Waldorf Astoria Hotel.

As Anthony Hyde, a management consultant living in London, opened the meeting, an ABC camera crew came into the room. "Where's Fritz Efaw?" shouted correspondent John Martin.

"Gentlemen," said Hyde, "do you agree this is our meeting? This is Convention business. Fritz has had his day. This is our business. Do you agree?"

"No," Martin said. "Where's Fritz Efaw?"

Efaw, in fact, was not there. He was being interviewed by CBS upstairs. He was electronic property, a celebrity: a draft evader under federal indictment who had fled the United States in 1969 to avoid service in Vietnam and had now returned for the first time, as an alternate delegate to the Convention. Television breeds and feeds on celebrity—and vice versa—and the cycle of electronic ecology was not about to be broken by the likes of Anthony Hyde and his "Convention business." "We want Efaw now. Where is he?"

"Let's watch Jimmy on 'Meet the Press,'" said Hamilton Jordan, Carter's 31-year-old campaign manager, fooling with the dials on the color set in room 2101 of the Americana at 12:30 on Sunday afternoon. Behind him, his wife, Nancy, was telling one of his assistants, Jim Langford, to save the rolls and butter from breakfast because they were just too expensive to throw out. Jordan had already passed out Cokes to visitors, saying: "Enjoy it. It's a dollar a bottle."

Trying to find Channel 4, the NBC station in New York, Jordan stopped on Channel 2, the CBS station, and saw William vanden Heuvel, Carter's New York coordinator, being interviewed on a local panel show called "Public Hearing." "Oh," Carter's man said without warmth, "vanden Heuvel's competing with Jimmy again. Let's watch this . . ."

There was a joke among the Secret Servicemen guarding Carter that they could take it easy in New York because, when there were photographers around, vanden Heuvel kept his face so close to the candidate's that if a gunman fired, "vanden Heuvel will take the bullet."

Intelligent and charming, vanden Heuvel was an exaggerated political type: the coat holder. He had never made it on his own but, loyal and possessed by demons of self-promotion, he had stayed close to a series of powerful men —working his way through General William ("Wild Bill") Donovan, the head of the Office of Secret Service in its transition to the Central Intelligence Agency, Senator Jacob Javits, Governor Averell Harriman, and the Kennedys, John and Robert. Then in the days of 1975, when Carter could get no one else, vanden Heuvel became the Georgian's man in New York. Before the Convention, vanden Heuvel was getting 200 telephone calls a day.

"The thing you have to know about me is that I'm not a political person, winning was never my bottom line—I went for Carter in 1975 because I thought he'd make a good president," vanden Heuvel told an interviewer, without mentioning that he had run, and lost, for governor, congressman, and Manhattan district attorney. A few minutes later, asked why he had not supported Senator

Birch Bayh, a friend, vanden Heuvel answered: "Because I didn't think he could win."

Vanden Heuvel arrived at the Americana about an hour after the competing television shows, wanting to see Carter and persuade him to go to a cocktail party being given that evening by Arthur Ochs Sulzberger, the publisher of the *New York Times*. Oh, to be the man who delivered Jimmy Carter to the *Times*! He got only as far as Jody Powell, the candidate's press secretary, one of the Carter-men who knew that the boss had given instructions that vanden Heuvel was to be kept away.

The coordinator made his pitch, then went to the second-floor Carter pressroom where he had arranged a job distributing issue literature for the lady in his life, Isabel Hyde—she was said to be as ambitious as he, but she was prettier, too; in fact, she was downright beautiful. Vanden Heuvel ran into Ken Auletta, a columnist for the *Village Voice,* who mentioned that he had been with Hamilton Jordan and they had seen "Public Hearing."

"Oh, did Hamilton see me?" vanden Heuvel said, grinning. "Good. That's good."

Annie, a 22-year-old prostitute who looked a little like a younger Diana Ross, had been busted 50 times by Lieutenant Gallagher's Public Morals Squad. Three of those times she went to jail, twice for 15 days and once for 30 days. But she expected a big week. She claimed to have made $800 a day during the 1972 Democratic National Convention in Miami Beach—and had given most of it to her pimp. Flying down from Boston—her family was from Dorchester, Massachusetts—she had worked Collins Avenue at night and spent the afternoons "creeping"— sneaking from cabana to cabana at hotel pools and stealing pocket cash and anything that glittered.

But in 1976, as the Convention was about to begin,

Annie was already feeling heat. Working Broadway and
47th on Saturday night, she had agreed to two $50 tricks
at hotels she knew well, the New York Hilton and the St.
Moritz. At both places, she was surprised by security men
who stepped in front of her in the lobby. Her customers
just ignored her, walking to the elevators. On the street,
there seemed to be cops everywhere, and she did a lot more
walking than usual, making $250, most of it from regular
West Side traffic. Sunday, she went to work at Eighth Avenue and 43rd Street, making $250 again—Convention or
no Convention, that was Annie's usual take for eight hours,
unless she got lucky and got her hands on a wallet.

The Americana Suite, rooms 2150 to 2154 in the hotel of
the same name, was less overdone than the rest of the place,
but the décor still bordered on Mafia Tasteful—the suite
had, in fact, been used in the filming of *The Godfather*. It
was the favorite of Frank Sinatra and had been used occasionally by John F. Kennedy. It was actually a penthouse
on top of one wing of the hotel. Unfortunately, Jimmy
Carter, the occupant this week, could not enjoy either the
views or New York's suspicious air. The Secret Service
had sealed off the balconies and insisted that curtains be
drawn because every room was within sight—and rifle
range—of thousands of skyscraper windows.

Carter was in the bookless "library" of the suite talking
with Representative Peter Rodino of New Jersey, one of the
seven men he said he was considering as his candidate for vice-president. Rodino, 67, was on the list for
cosmetic purposes, to impress other Italian-Americans and
to remind the country of his service as the chairman of the
House Judiciary hearings during Watergate impeachment
proceedings against former president Richard Nixon. Still,
the two men talked for 90 minutes, then went downstairs

to a second-floor pressroom and told 200 reporters everything but the truth.

Rodino had told Carter upstairs that he was not interested in the nomination—he knew it was not going to be
offered to him. Instead, the congressman wanted to give
the speech placing Carter's name in nominaton Wednesday
night. But the two politicians answered questions for 30
minutes, easily and smilingly discussing Rodino's qualifica-
tions for the office.

The press conference was one of the final acts in a
Carter production that was part public relations and part
common sense. The vice-president plan had been originally
designed to give newspapers and television something to
talk and write about—the theory being that idle reporters
are the devil's plaything during Convention Week. But it
had evolved into a serious attempt to avoid making the
kind of mistake that the last Democratic nominee, George
McGovern, had made in hastily selecting a running mate,
Senator Thomas Eagleton, who was dropped from the
ticket when it was revealed that he had been covering up a
history of mental problems.

Now the Georgian was making a show of interviewing
seven prospective running mates—Senators Walter Mondale, Edmund Muskie, and John Glenn had gone to Carter's home in Plains, Georgia, and Rodino and Senators
Frank Church, Henry Jackson, and Adlai Stevenson III
were being interviewed in New York. All seven had also
been asked to fill out a 17-question form (see Appendix B)
that asked them things like: "Have you ever had psychiatric
treatment?" . . . "Without details, is there or has there
been anything in your personal life which you feel, if
known, may be of embarrassment in the presidential election this year?"

"There is no way on earth people can take the vice-president of the United States seriously," Mondale had once told a newspaper columnist. He was now taking the whole thing very seriously indeed—his staff and Glenn's checked with the New York Telephone Company to find out the cost of installing special telephones so that Jimmy Carter would not get a busy signal if he decided to call them. The rate, they were told, was $229.49, even for one call—New York Tel's minimum installation was charged at commercial rates for a full month.

Like Hurley Goodall of Indiana, Patrick Sweeney, the assistant majority leader of the Ohio House of Representatives, was a Carter alternate and drove to New York. He made the trip in his leased 1976 Chevrolet Monte Carlo because he had a sister in New Jersey and figured he could get out to see her during the Convention. He parked the car on East 26th Street in front of the building where he was using a friend's apartment.

Late Sunday afternoon, Sweeney was walking back to the apartment after a long brunch at a neighborhood pub called Molly Malone's when he saw someone in his car. He stood and watched—and as the man backed out of the car with Sweeney's camera in his hand, Sweeney said, "Excuse me, have you got a match?" The man straightened up and Pat Sweeney, who was 37, weighed 230 pounds, and was once a Golden Gloves boxing champion, hit him with the hardest right cross he could throw.

The guy staggered against the car, and Sweeney pinned his arms there. "Hey, man," the thief said, "take it easy. I can't afford a bust. Don't call the cops. I'll pay you for the broken window."

"Well . . ." Sweeney hesitated, and the guy broke and ran. Sweeney ran after him, and he tackled the thief on the corner of 26th Street and Third Avenue, drawing a small crowd out of the Abbey Tavern.

"Hey, pick on somebody your own size," said one man, looking at the small thief struggling in Sweeney's arms.

"He broke into my car!"

"Oh. Then kill the motherfucker!"

Patrolmen Al Ryan and James Reed pulled up then in a NYPD patrol car, taking Sweeney and the thief to the 13th Precinct station house. The man gave his name as Roy Kisowski, age 32. "Why didn't you finish him off?" the desk sergeant said, looking at the blood on Kisowski. "It's less work to fill out a homicide report than an arrest card. You sure you want to press charges?"

"Yes."

"Okay. Be at the Criminal Court Building downtown at 9:30 tomorrow morning."

Jimmy Carter, who already had more than 2,000 invitations and interview requests, had never intended to go to Punch Sulzberger's party. His private schedule showed him spending three hours at a reception for Carter delegates at Pier 88 on the Hudson River. "Why do they have him in there for that long?" grumbled Evan Dobelle, the mayor of Pittsfield, Massachusetts, an early Carter supporter working the Convention on the candidate's personal staff.

James Gammill, Carter's 22-year-old Convention coordinator, told Dobelle: "Jimmy wanted it that way himself. I don't know why."

The candidate wanted to be on Pier 88 to shake the hand of each of the more than 1,800 delegates pledged to him. He wanted people to know—or he wanted to give the impression—that he personally cared about other human beings, one at a time. He was often called a media politician, but he actually practiced a kind of antimedia politics. When he arrived at 7:30, before any delegates, he stationed himself near the only entrance to the long, low pier, while his assistants whispered that the television cameras were set up at the far end. "That's their problem," Carter said; his was convincing these delegates and the people they would talk with for the next three months that Jimmy Carter wasn't above them all, wasn't part of the American alienation.

"Mazie," Carter said to a large black woman, "the last time we talked, you didn't have to stand in line like this. I owe all this to people like you."

Mazie Woodruff, a grandmother 13 times and a candidate for county commissioner back home in North Carolina, was thrilled that the candidate had remembered her. They had met only once before—in Winston-Salem in March—and she had been just as impressed then because he seemed comfortable with blacks, not fidgety like the white liberals from the North.

"Lucille," Carter said to another woman as the long line of delegates moved by him, "I've been waiting for you." He kissed Lucille Kelley, the 56-year-old chairwoman of the New Hampshire delegation. They had met and had lunch in Manchester more than two years before when he was campaigning for congressional candidates in her state, and they had talked for two and a half hours before she stood up and said: "Governor, you're the man I'd like to see in the White House two years from now."

Carter, who had never mentioned running for president, smiled. Two weeks after their meeting, he invited Miss Kelley, the former president of the Manchester Women's Democratic Club, to Atlanta for a ten-day visit with his family at the governor's mansion. When her brother died that November, Carter called and said he would fly up to Manchester if that would help, but she said no, that was not necessary. "You've already got our prayers, Lucille," Carter said. "We're on our knees tonight for you."

As Jimmy and Rosalynn Carter continued to greet delegates, many of them by their first names, a small man named Joseph Kaselak, from Lyndhurst, Ohio, stood just behind them, trying to be as unobtrusive as possible. He stayed next to a black Secret Service agent for 20 minutes, until he was sure that he was in most of the dozens of pictures being snapped off by a bobbing photographer from the *New York Daily News.*

Clare Smith, the youngest delegate, wanted to talk to Carter, but took one look at the lines for fried chicken and beer and decided that she had priorities—one of them was not to spend $2.50 for a New York hamburger. The lines looked to her like Food Stamp lines at home, except that the delegates were better dressed. The beer, however, did not run out and, like a lot of other people, Clare grabbed some to take back to her hotel. She put three six-packs under her arm and walked out, thinking that if her mother ever saw her . . . A UPI photographer appeared and got a picture of the youngest delegate. "Oh, God," Clare said to a friend.

Carter's press secretary, Jody Powell, and Patrick Caddell, the candidate's pollster, were dispatched to represent the candidate at the *Times*'s reception in the 14th floor offices of Punch Sulzberger. "Remember one thing," said Caddell, a 26-year-old survivor of George McGovern's disastrous 1972 campaign. "If we lose by five votes, these people will never invite us back."

Lucille Kelley from Manchester had also made the *Times*'s invitation list. At another party, she told Phyllis Cerf Wagner, the wife of former New York Mayor Robert Wagner, that she had forgotten to thank her hosts at the *Times.*

"You can do it now," said Mrs. Wagner. "They're right behind you."

"What are their names again?"

"Sulzberger," said Mrs. Wagner, "they're *very* important."

Inside Madison Square Garden, Judy Osteller of the Democratic National Committee was walking across the podium picking up yellow-tinted glass ashtrays and replacing them with 89-cent clear glass ones—the television networks had informed the DNC that the pale yellow ashtrays were distracting on camera (and so were yellow legal pads, which sent the DNC looking for white pads). Behind her, carpenters were driving the last nails into the sheetrock and fire-resistant plywood structure—some of it covering bulletproof lead plates—while four guards kept delegates away from the podium. The carpenters had complained that they were having trouble finishing because delegates kept coming up and taking their nails as souvenirs.

On the floor, workmen were getting ready to put up the symbols of the Convention—the 56 13-foot-high standards of the 50 states plus territories, the District of Columbia, and Democrats Abroad. The red-and-white standards, each with the name of a delegation—including a misspelled "Lousiana"—on the face of a wooden triangular prism, were to be slipped into aluminum sleeves attached to the first chair in each delegation.

The sleeves were tied to the folding chairs with plastic binders, which kept snapping if the 70-pound poles tilted. When the ties ran out, Garden workmen borrowed ties used by the New York Telephone Company to bind exposed bunches of phone cables. It looked fine—and satisfied Convention Manager Andrew Shea's insistence that the standards could be pumped up and down during demonstrations—even though Dick Donopria, the Garden's maintenance superintendent for more than 30 years, was unhappy, looking at the sharp-edged standards as if they were weapons. "I don't think they're safe—they should be bolted," Donopria told his boss, Arthur ("Mickey") Mc-Cauley, the executive vice-president of the Garden.

At 11:00 P.M. on Sunday, 24 people, most of them quite young, crowded into suite 2018 at the New York Sheraton, the rooms of Ohio's Lieutenant Governor Richard Celeste, the man who had brought Clare Smith and John Glenn together for photographers that afternoon. Jerry Austin, William Flaherty, and Jan Allen were three of the five members of Celeste's staff—the lieutenant governor of Ohio has almost no governmental responsibilities—and most of the rest were volunteers who had come in from Ohio on their own. Celeste groupies, Celestials.

Celeste assigned his people to the larger delegations—California, New York, Illinois, and down the line—telling them to get to know the delegates and leaders, hang around, pick up the gossip, meet in the suite after each Convention session, be ready. Be ready to push John Glenn for vice-president. Who knows? After he was nominated for president, Carter might decide to throw the vice-presidential nomination open to the floor. Celeste told them he had already set up a phone bank to use if there was any kind of fight—a friend, Jay Jacobson, head of the legal department at Saxon Industries at 450 Seventh Avenue, would let them use the company's offices and 12 telephones if they needed them. And remember, always introduce yourself as an aide of Dick Celeste and make a list of people you think might be leaders in their states or delegations in 1980, 1984.

When the others left, after midnight, Celeste and his wife, Dagmar, sat down to finish addressing 600 invitations to a cocktail party they were giving at the hotel on Wednesday night. Then they dropped invitations in hotel mailboxes around midtown. Hard work, but it might pay off in four years when Celeste expected to come back as governor of Ohio. And in eight years, Dick Celeste—one of the most attentive observers of the phenomenal rise of Jimmy Carter —planned to come back as a candidate for president of the United States.

At 10:00 P.M. on Sunday night, James McDonnell, the Democratic National Committee's security director, was putting the final touches on his plans for crowd control inside Madison Square Garden—and he realized that he needed 25 more ushers. McDonnell, who was taking leave as president of Andy Frain, Inc., had come up with the idea of using volunteers—"Convention aides"—as ushers and guards to save the $80,000 or so it would have cost to hire his company or one of its competitors in the crowd control business.

The only thing that anyone could think of to do at that point—22 hours before the Convention's first session—was to try to reach 50 men and women who had been among the 250 aides selected two months before from 600 applicants. These 50 had not been in contact with McDonnell's office after their original interview, and others had been chosen to take their places. This time, 35 of them answered their telephones and were told, as if nothing unusual were happening, that they should report to the "Orientation Meeting" in the Garden at midnight. Twenty-five came and were huddled together in a corner of the dim, eerie arena.

Mark Gasarch, a 34-year-old Manhattan attorney who had graduated from aide to aide-supervisor to one of the four aide-chiefs during earlier training sessions, volunteered to brief the midnight volunteers. After guiding the new aides around the Garden, he sat them down for final instructions at 2:00 A.M., and suddenly noticed a man, alone, walking around the empty floor—the Phantom of the Garden. In a while, the man came and sat behind the aides. It was Patrick Cunningham who, as New York State Democratic chairman and chairman of the DNC's Site Selection Committee, was the individual most entitled to claim that he had brought the Convention to New York City. Now, Cunningham was in disgrace, forced to take a leave as state chairman after being indicted for fixing judgeship appointments in return for bribes.

After Gasarch dismissed his new aides at 2:30 A.M., he looked back across the arena. Cunningham had moved and was sitting in the balcony, looking at the silent floor.

In 18 hours, across the hall from where Cunningham sat, Robert Strauss would call the Convention to order, repeating for the 37th time a ritual that began in Baltimore on May 21, 1832. President Andrew Jackson, who, like his predecessors, had been nominated by state legislatures and congressional caucuses, had called the first Democratic Convention to nominate Martin Van Buren as his running mate for vice-president in that year's election. Jackson seized on the convention—an idea originated the year before by the small Anti-Masonic party—as a device to dump his vice-president, John C. Calhoun.

Now, 144 years later, the party of Jackson was the oldest political organization in the world, the party that Bob Strauss had promised three and a half years ago to deliver to a candidate. On May 7, he had met with Jimmy Carter in Washington and said: "I've known for a long time that I'd have this conversation, but I never thought it would be so soon and I sure as hell never thought it would be with you. I am not the head of this party anymore. You are."

Unintentionally, though, the chairman had given Carter his first big boost toward the party's nomination. In 1974, Carter, still serving as governor of Georgia, had volunteered to take over as chairman of that year's Democratic National Campaign Committee, a job traditionally more title than work. But Carter took it very seriously, dispatching some of his most important assistants, including Hamilton Jordan, to Washington, and traveling throughout the country campaigning in almost every state for congressional candidates. In the middle of that effort, Robert Keefe, Strauss's chief political aide, told him: "Bob, this guy is running for president. He's using this to get an education on the issues and set up an organization." Still, Keefe and Strauss figured Carter was a 40-to-1 shot at best.

The Georgian, for his part, believed that Strauss's presidential favorites were his old friends, Senators Henry Jackson and Hubert Humphrey, who had helped make him national chairman in the first place. When the time came, one April night in Atlanta, to decide whether candidate Carter would keep Strauss on for the campaign, Carter snapped: "Why? He was against us?"

"Strauss *is* the Democratic party, Jimmy, we need him," someone argued.

Charles Kirbo, an Atlanta attorney who was Carter's closest friend and a man who liked the chairman, ended the argument by saying, "Bob Strauss will be loyal to whoever pays him." The wheeling Texas millionaire who actually took no salary from the DNC would have taken that as a compliment.

☒ **Monday**

July 12

"**W**e made it, Dottie!" Clare Smith said to her friend Dorothy Sievers, as they reached the floor of Madison Square Garden at 7:00 the first night. Later she wrote in her diary: "I was struck with awe."

It was an awesome sight: a huge bowl-shaped pinball machine, flashing with the color and light of 20,000 people involved in choosing the leader of their nation.

It was also a lousy place to hold the Convention. The floor space at the bottom of the five-story-high bowl was designed for the basketball and hockey heroics of the New York Knicks and the New York Rangers. So the 3,353 delegates and half-delegates were jammed into about 26,000 square feet. That made them more an audience than the milling, demonstrating, and dealing delegates of old. Space, or the lack of it, was an important element of control, which was exactly the way Chairman Strauss planned it. Besides that, the Garden building was round, and people kept getting lost. Even Andrew Shea, the 39-year-old Minneapolis lawyer who was the Convention manager, admitted that, after four months of roaming the building, he wasn't sure where he was 25 percent of the time.*

But the biggest problem with Madison Square Garden had nothing to do with room or with minor inconveniences like the fact that the building had only four public drinking fountains, none of them in public areas—a trick to increase beer and soft-drink sales during games. The real trouble was that the Garden was privately owned—it was, in effect, a subsidiary of the giant Gulf+Western Corporation, which owned 37.6 percent of Garden stock—while almost every other convention center in the country was municipally owned. And the City of New York, desperately trying to polish its corroded image, made its deal with the Democratic National Committee before even beginning to talk to Madison Square Garden Corporation about a contract.

Perhaps the city thought the Garden would be a municipal facility by Convention Week. A month after New York was selected as the Convention site on August 18, 1975, the *Village Voice,* a New York weekly, revealed that negotiations were almost completed for the sale of the Garden to the city's Off-Track Betting Corporation for $1 and then the leasing of the building back to Madison Square Garden Corporation for the same dollar bill. The effect of the sale would have been to remove the building from the city's real estate tax rolls—depriving New York, which was nearly bankrupt, of $2.5 million a year and increasing MSG's profits by the same amount. The whole thing stunk—the names of a dozen of the city's most prominent Democrats were attached to the deal—and the publicity killed it. But it also seemed to kill the Garden's enthusiasm for hosting Democratic delegates. "We have nothing

* There were usually between 5,000 and 7,000 people on the floor during Convention sessions. Many of them walked under a sign, hung on the podium camera platform, saying that, under various New York City codes, the maximum safe occupancy of the area was 2,476.

to do with the Convention," said James Appell, the Garden's executive vice-president, in January. "All we have to do, if the price is right, is to hand the key to the city."

By March, the city, the DNC, and the Convention were in trouble. No contracts for rental, design, or construction had been signed, and a new executive vice-president, Arthur ("Mickey") McCauley, had moved in as the Garden's negotiator. He began by telling New York and Democratic officials that if the six-month-old bargaining did not start from scratch with higher rental fees, the Garden would withdraw immediately—leaving the Democrats without a hall or a city.

"We do more preparation for a rock concert than you're doing right now," McCauley told the Democrats. "It was like dealing with entertainers," he said later. "You kid them and cajole them, or you stamp on their chests. . . . They didn't know what they were doing. Where were they from? Minnesota?"

Andy Shea, the Convention manager, was from Minnesota, and his main concern was keeping the troubles quiet—and he was tough and successful in doing that. On March 12, the convention staff got this memo from Shea: "Anyone who gets a call from the press should advise them that Vince [Clephas, the DNC's communications director] will speak to them. . . . In short, I do not want anyone but Vince speaking to the press without first having gone over it with Vince. I am sure you all understand that we speak to the press with one voice."

The one voice said everything was fine—covering up things like the fact that the Garden threw out New York Telephone Company workmen for two weeks in May when it was discovered that there was no insurance to cover them because the city was so far behind in premium payments. But after it was over, Shea said: "I was scared. New York is a frightening city. I had never met people like that.

Everything is a test of wills at first, whether you're dealing with the mayor or a cab driver. . . . I was baffled." *

But something had to be worked out—too many reputations were on the line—and in the line of publicity—if New York lost the Convention. The Democratic National Committee was almost as desperate as New York. Bob Strauss always felt he had been forced to come to New York—Miami Beach did not want another political convention and had already scheduled other events in its huge auditorium; New Orleans and Kansas City simply did not have enough hotel rooms; and Los Angeles—the city of angels was ruled out because the Democrats were convinced that the governor of California was crazy.

Edmund G. "Jerry" Brown, Jr., was not crazy at all. He was a clever politician with a talent, at least as impressive as Jimmy Carter's, for reaching people, especially young ones. Trading smartly on the name and connections of his father—former California Governor Pat Brown—he had barely won election in 1974, but had become phenomenally popular since. A former Jesuit seminarian who

* "As far as we were concerned, the Convention was in serious jeopardy of not being in New York until well into April," said the Garden's Mickey McCauley. "It was frightening. Until the contracts were signed on April 16, there were no plans and almost a total lack of real communication between the parties involved." One of those parties, CBS, maintained contingency hotel reservations in Los Angeles for its personnel until the end of May. There was also one false report—in the *New York Times* on January 18, 1976—that the Convention might move to Miami Beach. Preston Robert Tisch of the New York Host Committee, Daniel Courtenay of the New York Police Department, and Cliff Cassidy, chairman of the DNC Security Committee, were spotted in that city with James McDonnell and Miami Beach Police Chief Rocky Pomerance. What they were actually doing was combining a little business with a lot of pleasure—McDonnell, who was in charge of security for pro football's Super Bowl, had invited them to come down for the game in Miami instead of discussing Convention security in New York.

was inaugurated to the chants of a Sufi choir, Brown captivated Californians by circumventing liberal-conservative dogma and by wittily espousing an evolving, cerebral mix of the teachings of Saint Ignatius and Thomas Aquinas, Buddha, the existentialists, and Machiavelli.

So it was within the nature of Brown's political character that when the DNC Site Selection Committee went to Los Angeles in April, 1975, the Democratic governor casually attacked them as a bunch of big-time spenders looking for luxury hotels. He suggested that delegates should sleep in church basements. Mayor Thomas Bradley of Los Angeles, who was arranging parties at the homes of movie stars like Robert Wagner and Natalie Wood to impress the committee, was embarrassed. Governor Philip Noel of Rhode Island, a member of the committee, was enraged: "I will never vote to go anyplace that Jerry Brown has anything to do with. He accuses us of going to fancy parties—this dude who grew up in a governor's mansion while my mother was hitting a press in a jewelry factory. . . . The little bastard doesn't have a full seabag."

"It was New York by default," said Bob Strauss. "We are afraid of demonstrations and of getting caught up in the image of New York's financial and labor troubles. We desperately tried to figure out a way to go to New Orleans or Kansas City. . . . Miami Beach didn't want us again. And, then, that little bastard—I couldn't trust him. Who would go someplace where Jerry Brown controls the National Guard? I had visions of riots and him sitting on a mattress and refusing to call out troops."

With all of that, and with the sending of Knicks', Mets', and Yankees' uniform shirts to the sons of Site Selection Committee members, New York almost lost. The television networks were arguing so strongly for Los Angeles that Pat Cunningham, the New Yorker who was chairman of the committee, cracked: "You just want to get away from your wives for a few weeks at Malibu." On the day of the final vote, August 18, 1975, Governor Noel had two votes— he held a proxy for Senator Joseph Biden of Delaware— and that was the difference. The vote for New York was 11 to 9.*

Jerry Brown arrived in New York as a serious presidential candidate, having won 320 or so delegates in a series of spectacular late primary victories. He started too late to stop Carter—the Georgian was a declared candidate before Brown took office on January 1, 1975, and the Californian was forced to wait a while before flashing his ambition. But in the stretch, Brown badly embarrassed the front-runner. He out-Cartered Carter—Brown became the fresh face, the mysterious outsider, and Carter was the Establishment figure trying to consolidate his holdings. Even after Carter had clinched the nomination by winning the Ohio primary on June 8, Brown refused to quit, traveling the country needling the Georgian and picking up a few loose delegates here and there. Now, as usual, no one was sure what the hell Jerry Brown was going to do next.†

---

* After the vote, one committee member, Virginia Democratic party chairman Joseph Fitzpatrick, boasted privately that he had made the difference, saying he used his vote for New York to persuade Pat Cunningham to switch two New York congressional votes on an attempted override of President Ford's June, 1975, veto of legislation regulating strip-mining for coal. Fitzpatrick was, in fact, in Washington lobbying Democrats to oppose restrictions on strip-mining, an important industry in his part of Virginia. And two New York congressmen— Mario Biaggi and Samuel Stratton—did switch. The two New Yorkers voted for the bill and then immediately changed sides to support the president's veto, which was sustained by just three votes. Fitzpatrick, Cunningham, Stratton, and Biaggi denied there was a deal, saying that isn't the way politics works.

† Brown's name was on the ballot for only 4 primaries, beginning with Maryland on May 18—but he won 3 of those. He also campaigned for "Uncommitted" slates that won in two other states. Carter, on the other hand, entered 31 primaries, winning 18. The total vote, by candidate, in the primaries was: Carter—6,206,980; Brown—2,414,595; George

On Carter's floor of the Americana and on Strauss's floor of the Statler Hilton, the fear was that Brown would try to address the Convention and perhaps spark a movement for himself as the vice-presidential candidate. It was a measure of the pull of Brown's vague rhetoric about a new generation of leadership and planetary realism that both Strauss and Carter's senior adviser, Charles Kirbo, agreed that everything possible should be done to prevent Jerry Brown from getting near the podium.

"Let's just wait," Strauss said. "We'll keep our hands off. He's like a pimple on your face. If you touch 'em too soon, you get a red blotch. If you wait till the right moment, they just pop."

It was 8:00 P.M.—time to go to work. Morton Dean, one of CBS's four senior floor correspondents, turned to his relief correspondent, Lesley Stahl, and said off-camera: "Lesley, remember those waste bags the astronauts had? I'm wearing one of them. I won't have to come off the floor to go to the bathroom for 28 days." Sixty feet below them, two New York policemen stared at each other under a single 60-watt lightbulb in a soot-lined 30-by-40-foot chamber containing the main electrical lines and switching equipment for Madison Square Garden and Pennsylvania Station —their job was to make sure no one got near the transformers, switches, and fuses in their silent post at the end of a maze of tunnels whose entry doors had been spot-welded shut. In hidden nooks above each of the Garden's entrances, guards watched the approaching crowds through the ultraviolet light of football-sized Retroflective Scopes

---

Wallace—1,994,689; Udall—1,601,763; Jackson—1,133,941; Church—843,339; Robert Byrd—321,667; Sargent Shriver—304,394; Ellen Mc-Cormack—238,862; Fred Harris—234,554; Milton Shapp—52,642; Birch Bayh—47,959. (The chronology of Democratic delegate selection appears as Appendix A.)

that could spot counterfeit credentials 50 yards away—before delegates, guests, and reporters came near guards at the doorways or the Secret Servicemen, Customs officers, and Treasury agents standing behind each column on every one of the Garden's nine levels. On the eighth level, Robert Keefe, who had gone from executive director of the Democratic National Committee to become manager of Senator Henry Jackson's presidential campaign, scanned the floor of the arena with binoculars from the CBS anchor booth— he was being paid $3,500 for the week as a "spotter," looking for faces that would make interesting interviews for Mort Dean and his three roving partners. Across the hall, Mark Shields, a political consultant and, for a time, Mo Udall's manager, did the same thing for NBC.

Behind the podium, Tom Murray, a 28-year-old sportswriter who had volunteered as a Convention aide to find out how things worked, found out right away. He had his orders, simple: No one was to pass him without a 7-by-3-inch cardboard credential marked "Officer of the Convention" or "Podium." At 8:00, Bob Strauss, wearing nothing around his neck but a tie, walked out of his Garden office —usually the dressing room of visiting National Basketball Association teams—and walked right by the speechless aide.

At 8:15, the chairman banged his gavel for a minute, calling to order the Thirty-seventh National Convention of the Democratic Party of the United States. The number of gavel strokes was important. A television consultant— Eric Lieber, the producer of the "Sammy Davis Show"— had viewed films of the 1972 Convention and advised Strauss that more than four hours had been spent banging the thing and calling for order in Miami Beach, accomplishing nothing but to remind the television audience that there was disorder. The chairman wanted no disorder and no impression of disorder at his Convention and commanded that, no matter what was happening on the floor, gavel banging was to be restricted to three times a session, no more than a minute at a time.

The chairman stood over 3,353 delegates and half-delegates, the men and women with a total of 3,008 votes who would select candidates for president and vice-president and write, or ratify, the rules and platform of the Democratic party. He looked at two television cameras 60 feet in front of him on a 27-foot-high steel platform in the center of the floor between the Kentucky and Wisconsin delegations.

The men and women below Strauss constituted the majority party of the largest and most powerful democracy in the world, a political organism that traced its heritage through Franklin D. Roosevelt and Andrew Jackson to the author of the Declaration of Independence, Thomas Jefferson. It was no small thing to be there. They were the majority because they could fairly claim to be America. Their national rival for 120 years, the Republican party, was declining into a parody of the nation and its politics, an aging clustering of white Protestants, small tycoons, and shopkeepers from small places representing, according to polls, 20 percent or less of the American people. The party of Abraham Lincoln and Theodore Roosevelt had deteriorated into a reactive core that lived off Democratic mistakes, which were many—so many that the Republicans had controlled the focus of national power, the presidency, for eight years. Whatever else was true of the Democratic party, it was the chosen political vessel of 17-year-old Clare Smith and 84-year-old Averell Harriman whose father's railroad, the Union Pacific, had raped, and had helped build, the country; of Mazie Woodruff and Albert ("Dapper") O'Neil of Boston who had come to New York to argue that busing black children into his neighborhood was destroying his city; of George Wallace and Bella Abzug, and Tom Hayden and George Meany.*

By nature and history the Democrats were a cantankerous bunch. But Bob Strauss had spent three and a half years carefully binding them inside a webby structure of rules and committees and meetings and agendas. He planned to use them as a studio audience.

The Democrats were also the chosen party of Joe Kaselak, who was in New York for no other reason than to get on the floor of the Convention and get his very ordinary face in newspapers and on television. He had been up at seven o'clock that morning and on Lexington Avenue ten minutes later looking for a *Daily News*. He found the paper, but not what he was looking for. The photograph of Carter greeting delegates at the pier was on the front page—showing the candidate, the black Secret Service agent, and the corner of Kaselak's elbow.

His camera crashing started in 1960 when Kaselak, a state motor vehicle inspector who hung around politics, had hitched a ride to the Los Angeles Convention on the Ohio

---

* The Democratic delegates' differences with the nation, according to statistical analyses by the Associated Press and the *Washington Post*, were unsurprising: They were more male, better educated, and made more money. By sex, they were 66 percent male and 34 percent female. By age, they averaged about 43, with 14 percent under 30 and only 5 percent over 65. By race, 11 percent were black; 4.5 percent had Hispanic surnames. By religion, 48 percent were Protestant, 39 percent Roman Catholic, 8 percent Jewish. By education, 65 percent were college graduates, and only 2 percent had not completed high school. By income, 6 percent earned less than $10,000 a year; 19 percent earned between $10,000 and $18,000; 34 percent between $18,000 and $30,000; 22 percent between $30,000 and $50,000; and 19 percent more than $50,000. By ideology, 1 percent identified themselves as "radical," 55 percent as "liberal," 31 percent as "moderate," and 13 perecnt as "conservative."

delegation's chartered plane and had ended up on television standing, quite by accident, between two of John F. Kennedy's sisters. When he got home to Lyndhurst, that was all his friends talked about—Joe was on television, you know! Since then, he had caught on with Representative Charles Vanik as a driver and handyman to have around back in the district, and he had crashed every Convention, getting on television over and over again—usually on NBC, the network he told his family and friends to watch. In 1964, at Atlantic City, he had slipped into the line with members of Lyndon Johnson's $1,000-a-head "President's Club," giving the name of a Cleveland millionaire he knew had not yet arrived. In 1968, when Chicago security was extraordinarily tight, he was an Alabama delegate—or at least he had delegate credentials, having followed angry anti-Humphrey southerners when they walked off the floor and grabbed the tags of a disgusted Alabaman in a parking lot outside the hall. And in 1972 in Miami Beach, he had begged "Photographer's Assistant" credentials from a friend who was taking pictures for the Democratic National Committee.

But the past was prologue, and this time he had nothing but a free apartment at Lexington and 46th Street, the New York sleeping place of a Cleveland businessman who thought Joe—with his cigars, leisure suits, and white patent leather loafers—was a funny guy. But he was a tired funny guy. Kaselak was 57 years old and had spent three 16-hour days hanging around hotels trying to scrounge up the magic paper that would get him on the floor—and now some picture editor at the *News* had screwed him.

While Joe Kaselak was looking for his picture in the papers, a line of 11 blue-and-white New York Police Department patrol cars pulled up to the main entrance of Madison Square Garden. Thirty men and women, volunteer couriers, walked to the cars carrying canvas *New York Times* delivery bags over their shoulders. Inside the bags were what Joe Kaselak wanted: the credentials to the Convention.

The credentials, multicolored tags worn around the neck with an elastic string, were the coin of the Convention. They were counted and computerized by number and holder each day before the couriers began their appointed, guarded rounds. At the hotels where the chairmen or representatives of each of the 56 state and territorial delegations waited, the tags were counted again. The same ritual took place at other credential destinations—the offices of Governor Hugh Carey and Mayor Abraham Beame, Jimmy Carter headquarters, and the four Statler Hilton offices used to distribute tags each morning to authorized representatives of newspapers, magazines, radio and television news departments, and foreign publications.

Officially, there were 26,594 credentials distributed each day, from the most prestigious, "Officer of the Convention" —10 to 15 were issued daily to people allowed anywhere in the Garden—to the least prestigious, 3,000 "Guest" passes providing seats in the highest, smokiest galleries. Actually the number given out was 30,123—overruns were hidden from everyone but a few of the highest party officials, to allow the Democratic National Committee and Bob Strauss, a man of many friends and favors, to satisfy extra or unexpected politicians and reporters.*

---

* The daily credential classifications and numbers actually available were: Delegate, 3,353; Alternate, 2,086; DNC Member, 399; U.S. Senator, 68; U.S. Representative, 321; Governor, 42; Lt. Governor, 39; Guest, 3,600; Honored Guest, 6,600; News, 5,200; Officer of the Convention, 50; Staff, 550; Security, 1,500; Podium, 1,000; Floor, 1,500; Page, 165; Messenger, 500; Operations, 3,000; Orchestra, 150. There were actually only 37 Democratic governors—and similarly smaller numbers of other real elected officials—so five pseudogovernors could be walking around at any time. One midwestern newspaper reporter wearing a "Lt. Gover-

The printing of the credentials had begun on May 10 at Sterling Graphic Arts on East 45th Street in Manhattan. The paper stock used was available only in small quantities in the Midwest, to make counterfeiting more difficult in the city with the greatest printing capacity, legal and illegal, in the world. Three laminated layers of paper were used so that security personnel could tear tags to discover phonies by the absence of a blue middle layer. Under U.S. Secret Service protection, the bundles of credentials were moved in New York police cars to a second printing firm for perforation and then flown to Minneapolis in a private jet owned by Minnesota Mining and Manufacturing Company. At 3M, an inch-wide strip of "Retroreflective" paper was pasted to each tag so that the invisible letters "DNC" would show up when the strip was lit by Retroreflective viewers carried by security personnel. The bundles were then flown back to New York, and Sterling Graphics printed credential designations on the 3M strip. On June 24, the Secret Service locked the credentials in a security room at Madison Square Garden.

Only two people, DNC officials George Dillman and Kitty Halpin, had keys to the storage area. At midnight on the Saturday before the Convention, as a security check, Miss Halpin dialed the number of the telephone in the storage room. A man answered, laughing, and said: "Johnson's Funeral Home." Grabbing a Burns guard hired by the DNC, she ran from her office in the Statler Hilton across

---

nor of California" tag turned down an interview request from a British Broadcasting Corporation correspondent. In addition to the daily passes, 12,500 four-day credentials were issued—11,000 "News-Perimeter" allowing access only to press working areas and 1,500 "Service" for people like concession-stand attendants. Theoretically, 42,623 people could have been in Madison Square Garden, an arena basically designed to handle 19,500 spectators for a two-hour sporting event or show.

Seventh Avenue to the Garden. She and her guard were stopped by Garden guards who refused to let the Burns man into the building—union rule. By the time Miss Halpin got to the storage room, there was no one there.

New York City was a "union town." A lot of people who had read that phrase in newspapers never really understood what it meant until they hit the Big Apple—or it hit them. Like Sid Davis, the Washington Bureau chief of Westinghouse Group Broadcasting.

Davis came to New York on June 28—to be precise, at 2:00 P.M., June 28. He had to be precise because one of the more than a dozen memos he carried from the Democratic National Committee had informed him that Madison Square Garden had only one truck ramp and one freight elevator and that Westinghouse was scheduled to use them from 2:00 to 3:00 P.M. to unload the prefabricated offices for their seven radio and five television stations.

"Prefabricated offices" was a euphemism for a 20-by-11-foot wooden box, shipped in 8-by-4-foot sections from Philadelphia, where it had been built at a cost of $1,400. Westinghouse would have preferred to build the thing in New York, but the cost for the same work there was bid at over $6,000. Davis hired a Teamster crew to deliver the panels because one of his DNC memos warned: "You are advised to use only trucking companies that employ members of the Teamsters Union. It is possible that MSG personnel may not unload trucks which are not driven by Teamsters."

He had, it seemed, the wrong Teamsters. As Davis's truck pulled up to the Garden ramp on West 33rd Street, it was stopped by two men. "The local sent us to unload this truck," one said, identifying himself as a New York Teamster.

"Wait a minute," Davis said, "I've got a crew . . ."

"Hey!" a new arrival shouted. "Get away from there. That's carpenter's work."

Davis, a slight man of 5-foot-9, was literally in over his head. He retreated into the Garden, looking for someone in authority, finally finding Charles Uribe of A-J Contracting Company, the overall contractor for the Convention. They worked out a New York compromise—three Teamsters would be paid for an hour's work to move the panels from the front to the back of the Westinghouse truck, which was too large to use the ramp. Then the Carpenters Union would take them into the Garden at a billing rate of $18.22 an hour per man.

After the Teamsters did their job and left, the carpenters' chief said: "It's too heavy, we can't handle it."

Davis ran back into the Garden, found a man with a small dump truck, and paid him $50 to run the panels up the ramp. He told Uribe the panels were ready to be put together; under its contracts with the DNC and the city, only A-J Contracting could bolt the panels together.

"Good," Uribe said. "We can't do it today, though. It's after three-thirty, and my men are on overtime."

Dammit, Davis said, we had a contract, and I followed it to the letter—and I can't keep my men overnight in New York. Uribe sent his secretary out for the contract: Okay! It took A-J's carpenters four hours, at $32.32 an hour for each man, to assemble the panels; it had taken one hour to do the same work in Philadelphia.

Davis left for Philadelphia at 8:00 P.M. His day in New York had cost Westinghouse $1,800.

Ann Pincus, an aspiring journalist and a Washington hostess of some note, was riding down an elevator in the Americana at 9:30 that morning when someone introduced her to Hamilton Jordan, Carter's campaign manager.

"We'll be getting to know each other much better in Washington," she said with a smile. "By the way, are you called *Jor*dan or *Jer*dan?"

"My friends call me Jerdan," he answered. "But you can call me Jordan."

In suite 2018 of the Sheraton, Dick Celeste was writing invitations again—not to his own Wednesday night party this time, but to a smaller party that three important Ohioans wanted to give for John Glenn after his keynote speech on the Convention's opening night. Paul Tipps, the state Democratic chairman, had called Celeste in the morning and asked him to come up to his 24th-floor suite to talk with Steven Kovacik, a Columbus lawyer who had been Glenn's Senate campaign manager, and Marvin Warner, a Cincinnati real estate developer and part-owner of the National Football League's Tampa Bay Buccaneers. They wanted the first string—Walter Cronkite, people like that. Celeste had a staff, could he handle it? Of course.

When Celeste went off to a meeting of the Rules Committee, his assistant, Jerry Austin, and six Celestials began delivering 60 invitations by hand, saving the top 20—Cronkite, John D. Rockefeller IV, and others—for personal calls from the hustling lieutenant governor. Then the *Plain Dealer*s came, 200 copies of the Cleveland newspaper, which were stamped "Compliments of Lt. Governor Dick Celeste" and handed to the most important Ohioans in New York. Those 200 people had already received, by mail before the Convention, Dick Celeste's four-page "Suggestions for Your New York Visit" listing sights and transportation facilities near the Sheraton and recommending that they try the cream-cheese-on-raisin-bread sandwich at Chock Full O'Nuts on West 49th Street.

All of this was too much for some people, and a mysterious raider kept ripping down the signs that Celestials put up: "Rumors Originated and Circulated—Celeste Suite 2018. Feel Free to Share Your Daily Discoveries. Call or Stop By." But Celeste had been preparing for this week for almost a year. On February 7, he had called a meeting at Ohio State University to brief his followers on how to become delegate candidates in the state's June 8 primary election; invitations had gone out to the 12,000 names he had collected on a personal list he had begun compiling when his father was mayor of Lakewood, a Cleveland suburb. Three hundred men and women had come on a bitter, snowy day—more than 100 of them became candidates, and 40 were in New York as delegates and alternates for Carter or Udall. Celeste's 30-year-old brother, Ted, ended up as Carter's state campaign chairman, and two of the five people on the lieutenant governor's payroll—Jerry Austin and Bill Flaherty—took leaves to work for Udall. Dick Celeste never committed himself; he was not a delegate, just a concerned citizen trying to be helpful—like Jimmy Carter.

✓ Celeste lived the same kind of life or nonlife as the candidate, totally disciplined—he fasted every Wednesday to remind himself, he said, that there were hungry people in this world—campaigning every day and night at county fairs and Rotary lunches in the same uniform of blue blazer, buttondown oxford shirt, and Bass Weejun loafers. He looked more Yale '59 and Rhodes scholar—he was both, and had also been Chester Bowles's assistant in the U.S. embassy in India for four years—than the son of Francesco Palma Celeste, who came from Calabria, Italy, to make his fortune in the New World. Frank Celeste did make a lot of money building apartment houses, then became mayor of Lakewood and raised his children as Methodists.

State Representative Larry Morris, a delegate from Alexander City, Alabama, was walking across the lobby of the New York Hilton at about 11:00 A.M. when he saw George Wallace's brother, Gerald, and campaign manager, Charles Snider. "I'm having a hard time bringing myself to vote for Carter," he said. "That's not what the folks back home elected me to do—they voted for George Wallace."

"The governor doesn't want to cause ripples," Snider said. Gerald Wallace added that his brother wanted to leave New York with dignity.

George Wallace had been sending ripples across the United States since he was elected governor of Alabama as a segregationist and had stood in the doorway of the state university for a couple of televised minutes to briefly block the entry of its first black student. In 1976, he had run for president for the fourth time, campaigning in a wheelchair because of the paralyzing effects of a would-be assassin's bullet during his 1972 campaign. After carrying five southern states as an independent candidate in 1968 and winning a string of Democratic primaries before being shot in 1972, Wallace had tried desperately to convince voters that he could physically handle the presidency. He failed—mostly because of Jimmy Carter. The Georgian began campaigning as an enlightened alternative to Wallace, collecting northern supporters to help him topple Wallace in the Florida primary—and Carter did that, barely defeating Wallace in the first southern primary of 1976.*

* The Florida vote on March 9, 1976, was: Carter—439,870; Wallace—392,105; Senator Henry Jackson—306,120. The result told a good deal about American politicians and why many people had become disillusioned about established leaders. Jackson decided to enter the Florida race only three weeks before the election, apparently with the encouragement of Senator Hubert Humphrey, who gave him permission to use old Humphrey tapes as radio commercials. The only reason for the late entry seemed to be an effort to cut Carter's vote—up to that point, it appeared that Carter would win by a large margin. Given a choice, Jackson and Humphrey seemed to prefer the survival of Wallace, whom they would privately say was a threat to the country, to the survival of Carter, who was rapidly becoming a threat to their own ambitions.

After Carter won the Ohio primary on June 8, Wallace endorsed the Georgian, trying to present Carter as the natural heir to his efforts and ideas—which, to a certain extent, was a fact. At the Alabama delegation party on Sunday night, Ray Jenkins, the editorial page editor of the *Alabama Journal,* a persistent and perceptive Wallace critic, said: "If Wallace had been well, he would have won Florida . . . and Carter would have been the one who was finished. As it is, the only thing Wallace has left to fight for is his self-respect, and the only way he can rationalize these twelve years is by throwing his full support behind Carter. . . . The only real difference between Wallace and Carter is fifteen years. They both started out in politics as opportunists with slight liberal inclinations. The only way for Wallace to get elected governor in 1962 was as a segregationist, but that made it impossible for him to command real nationwide support. By the time Carter became governor of Georgia in 1970, the Civil Rights Act and the Voting Rights Act had made it possible to get elected in the South without mortgaging your future to the rednecks. The person Jimmy Carter has to thank is not George Wallace—it's Lyndon Johnson."

Before going to Madison Square Garden, Clare Smith had done four filmed television interviews and appeared on the "Midday!" show on New York's Channel 5—besides being followed by Bob Dotson and a film crew from Cleveland's Channel 3 for "A Day with the Youngest Delegate." She had also sold her "Guest" pass for the night's session for $10 to a Cleveland businessman and fundraiser named Robert Black.

"Ready with the apples," Bob Dotson said after filming some shopping by Clare and her friend, Beth Farnsworth, a Carter delegate who was a few months older. The camera zoomed in on Dotson with a microphone in one hand and

an apple in the other as Clare and Beth took bites on cue:
". . . and now the girls have had their first taste of the
Big Apple."

On her way out of the Ohio caucus that afternoon, Clare
was stopped by a reporter from the Sun Newspapers, a
suburban chain in Ohio, and three photographers con-
verged on her. "Oh, Beth," she said, "wait and then we'll
get the film." The youngest delegate needed film for her
own camera. What kind? Each of the photographers handed
her a free can.

"Bombs!" yelled Dan Meenan. "There are bombs going
off all around town." Meenan, a reporter for WMCA
radio in New York, was leading the charge of a dozen
reporters out the 33rd Street side of Madison Square Garden.
Ten small firebombs had gone off just before 1:00 P.M.
in six large stores, including R. H. Macy's and Gimbel's on
Herald Square, a block from the Garden.

"Today, July 12," said a note found in a telephone booth,
"the armed commando unit Andre Figueroa Cordero det-
onated 12 incendiary bombs. . . . This is in protest of
the presence of 22 colonial leeches attending the national
convention of one of the ruling political parties of the
United States."

The FALN (Armed Forces of National Liberation) was
a Puerto Rican terrorist group that claimed credit for a
series of New York bombings, including one that killed five
people in Fraunces Tavern near Wall Street, and it was the
principal worry of Dan Courtenay, the ranking New York
police officer at the Convention. The NYPD had never been
able to infiltrate the FALN and, in fact, was not sure
exactly what it was, but street informants had been saying
for months that the Convention—particularly the 22 delegates from Puerto Rico—was an FALN target.

"You cannot totally secure this building without searching every person who comes in," said Courtenay, who commanded 1,500 cops assigned to the Convention, 1,100 of them in and around the Garden. "That's obviously impossible, so it will not be hard to get bombs in there—plastic, carrying the parts separately. The best defense is keeping your eyes open."

Your eyes and Sally's. At that moment, Sally, a nine-year-old black Labrador retriever, was being walked through the seats of the New Jersey delegation by a New York patrolman, Ronald McLean. Sally, who was being kept in a van parked on the Garden's main ramp, was a NYPD bomb sniffer—she and a German shepherd partner named Brandy were just about the only way of finding plastic bombs, which had no metal parts. The dogs' sense of smell was supposed to be seven times better than human noses, and they were trained daily by searching for hidden sticks of dynamite and were rewarded with dog biscuits when they found them.

The night before, in an eight-hour sweep of the building from the roof to the subbasement, an Army Explosives Ordnance Disposal team had found a device hidden in a filing cabinet in a first-floor office. With bomb threats already coming in at a rate of more than a dozen a day, Dan Courtenay and Richard Jordan, the Secret Service agent in charge, were called in to examine the timer, a small clock taped to a Coca-Cola can. It was a phony. Within two hours, it had been traced to a television reporter who planned to do a story on how he had fooled the Secret Service. He was told that if he tried to fool them again, he might be doing stories from Leavenworth, Kansas.

Jordan, who was in charge of the Secret Service's Chicago office, had worked his first convention in 1960, guarding Vice-President Richard Nixon. He had begun poring over blueprints of Madison Square Garden in November and had moved into a New York apartment on June 1. Riding in from La Guardia Airport that day, his cab driver said: "You know, the Democratic Convention is coming to town next month."

"Sure," Jordna said, "I just read something in the paper about it."

"I guess they're expecting trouble."

"Is that right?"

"Yeah," the cabbie said, "I hear they're gonna build an electric fence around Madison Square Garden. If you try to get over it, it won't kill you, just hurt you."

The Secret Service agent thought to himself: "Just keep thinking that, baby. Spread the word."

Sal Lividini hoped the Convention and publicity would somehow change things at the old 1,800-room Statler Hilton. "There are three rules for running a good hotel," he said, "location, location, and location." For 20 years, as the trains stopped running to Penn Station, the Statler had had a lousy location. But this week, he had the best location in the world, with television cameras ringing the building and the lobby.

But instead of being on television—and attracting the attention that might get him the first-line Hilton hotel he wanted—the little manager was being nibbled to death by stuck elevators and escalators, Hare Krishna beggars slipping in and out of the lobby like bald moths, and one bomb threat after another. Some of the bomb threats coming to John Sabo, the day assistant manager stationed at a desk in the middle of the crowded lobby, were coming from phones inside the house: "Some delegates!"

Besides all that, the newspapers and magazines renting office space on the hotel's mezzanine were complaining about being robbed blind. Neither the Statler Hilton nor the Democratic National Committee had provided security guards for the temporary offices, open space marked off by blue curtains hanging from pipe racks. At 11:30 A.M. on Friday, Helen McCosker of the Cox Newspapers signed for three rented televisions and had them placed on a table while she went around the corner to pick up a press release. When she got back, there were two televisions—she looked at her watch and saw it was 11:32. A half hour later, Arthur Wiese of the *Houston Post* returned to his cubicle after a 15-minute errand and discovered his typewriter was gone. A reporter's handbag with $200 and credentials was taken from the *Houston Chronicle* in the next booth. The *Washington Post* lost two $800 IBM electric typewriters on Friday and another on Saturday. The *Toledo Blade* had a hotel television installed that day at 1:00 P.M. It was gone by 2:00. The TV stand lasted until 5:00. Lividini's assistants gave Wiese of the *Houston Post* some advice: Don't bother to report the thefts to the police. In New York, they usually don't check out burglaries.

For weeks, smaller newspapers had been complaining about another "New York ripoff." The original DNC price list indicated that it would cost newspapers from five to ten times as much to rent equipment in New York as it had in Miami Beach in 1972. Televisions were quoted at $50 a day, plus delivery charges, plus installation; the blue curtains were quoted at $15 per linear foot. In Kansas City, where the Republicans were holding their Convention, television rental was $16 a week and drapes $3 a foot. The *Washington Star* paid $1,200 in New York to rent a large desk, seven tables, eight chairs, four wastebaskets, and six typewriters. "We'll get these costs down," Chairman Strauss assured Ronald Sarro of the *Star,* "if I have to kill every goddamned son-of-a-bitch in New York trying . . . It's not the money, but the principle involved, that's important."

"Excuse me, Mr. Chairman," Sarro replied. "It *is* the money. Screw principle."

Pat Sweeney, the Ohio legislator who wanted to press charges against the man who broke into his car, was at Criminal Court before nine o'clock. A policeman on duty outside the courthouse on Centre Street showed him where to park his Monte Carlo with its smashed side window.

Inside, he filled out reports with Patrolman Ryan, the officer who had arrested the thief, and a woman from the Manhattan district attorney's office. They told him that Roy Kisowski would probably be charged with larceny, a felony, but that if he agreed to plead guilty—"plea bargaining," it was called—the charge would be dropped to a misdemeanor. It was two o'clock in the afternoon before Sweeney finished and went back outside to the space where the cop had told him to park.

Sweeney's car was gone; it had been towed away. "See, it's a 'Towaway Zone,'" Ryan said, pointing to a "No Parking" sign. The Ohioan took a taxi to the car pound on an old Hudson River pier on the other side of Manhattan.

"That'll cost you sixty-five dollars," said the cop in the cubicle at the pound. "Let me see your registration."

The registration was at the car-leasing company in Lancaster, Ohio. Sorry, pal. No registration, no car.

At 3:45, New York Congressman Charles Rangel came out of one of the Statler Hilton's renovated meeting rooms, the Georgian Room, and was surrounded by reporters. What's the fighting about? What do you want from Carter? "Our problem with the governor is," said the Harlem legislator, a leader of the Black Caucus, "is that, uh, our problem, uh, we have no problems."

In fact, the caucus of black delegates and elected officials had been inside for almost two hours debating whether to demand reinstatement of quotas for black delegates—mandatory racial percentages had been eliminated under Strauss's new rules—and whether to enforce their demands by threatening to nominate a black candidate for president or vice-president to disrupt the Convention's aggressive unity.*

But they were doing it behind closed doors. Mazie Woodruff, the North Carolina grandmother who had met Jimmy Carter for the second time the night before, was one of those who argued for throwing reporters out before getting down to business. The essence of the press's business —what it calls "News"—is change and conflict. If you want change or trouble, keep them around—reporters, by their nature, tend to find or foster confrontation. "If we have an argument in our own house and then come out happy and together, then everything's all right," Mrs. Woodruff said. "But if someone is in here, they might go out and quote first one and then the other, and then things grow and become a problem. We don't want that this time."

That's the way it was. Mazie Woodruff, a shipping clerk, was prevailing over Charlie Rangel, a congressman. Mrs. Woodruff was for Carter and unity; Rangel, a Udall supporter, had been practicing the politics of demands for decades. And the Rangels were not sure how far they could go this time, because in the primaries black voters had generally supported Jimmy Carter, a candidate northern black leaders did not support, did not even know. Black "spokesmen" and the people they usually spoke to, the

---

* The Democrats are almost unchallenged as the party of black America, usually winning more than 90 percent of the black vote. Partly because of that, the party introduced delegate quotas for minority groups, as well as youth and women, after the 1968 Convention, when 5.5 percent of the delegates were black, compared with an 11 percent share of the country's population. In 1972, with quotas, 15 percent of the delegates were black. In 1976, the figure was 11 percent.

press, were partners in frustration—no demands and damned few stories.

By late afternoon, empty-handed, Joe Kaselak decided he had to call his employer, Congressman Vanik—even though Kaselak's job in Vanik's Cleveland office had nowhere near enough status to claim one of the congressman's allotment of two "Guest" credentials.

"Are you coming tonight?" Kaselak asked.

"I don't know. My wife's too sick to come," Vanik said from Washington.

"Boss, can I have her ticket?"

"The governor is ready to enter the room. But before he comes in, we want some decorum here. Let's show some respect."

George Wallace was wheeled in before 300 delegates pledged to him from Alabama, Massachusetts, Wisconsin, Florida, North Carolina, and a dozen other states, at 6:35 P.M. There was no decorum; the meeting room at the New York Hilton went crazy with applause, cheers, yells, and chants for three minutes.

"It sounds like I ought to say, 'I accept your nomination,'" the man in the wheelchair said, and there was another four minutes of stomping.

Larry Morris, the Alabama state representative who acted as Wallace's floor leader in the legislature, was leaning against the back wall with his arms folded across his chest. He was depressed and disgusted. "If they had put this much energy into the campaign," he said, looking at the jumping, fist-waving crowd, "we wouldn't be in the sad shape we are. It's like raisin' sand after the ballgame is over."

"Now I know some of you want to vote for George Wallace on Wednesday night, and technically I'm still a candidate, but . . ."—there were more cheers—"but I want you to vote for Carter and give the party bosses a taste of their own medicine. After Florida, I got calls from the hierarchy all over the U.S.A., people who wouldn't deign to speak to me before, praising my courage and telling me that I have written an important page in the history books. Their aim was to encourage me to stay in the race and use my delegates to get a deadlocked Convention which they could broker in their smoke-filled rooms. They wanted to use George Wallace to stop Jimmy Carter, just as they had used Jimmy Carter to stop George Wallace. . . . They thought they could look down their noses at me and still use me to deprive a southerner of the nomination.*

"I still ask you to vote for Carter, but if you don't go along, I'll still respect you. I hope this country is on the way to being straightened out, and we're the ones who did it. I love you all. God bless you."

If you don't go along, I'll still respect you. Larry Morris wondered whether there still might be something for him in this damn Convention. So far, all Morris had gotten for coming to New York were two television interviews—with WAPI from Birmingham and WCOV from Montgomery. What if Wallace agreed to have his name placed in nomination, and what if Larry Morris were the man to do it—on national television?

Mazie Woodruff decided to walk the 24 blocks from the New York Hilton Hotel to Madison Square Garden—partly to save money. The Holladay family, for whom she had worked 16 years, first as a maid, then as a clerk, had paid

---

* Wallace aides later identified the callers from "the hierarchy" as Democratic Chairman Strauss, Senator Hubert Humphrey, and former California Governor Edmund G. ("Pat") Brown, who would have had his son's interests at heart.

most of her way to New York. But she also wanted to walk to see and hear the city she had been sure would be nothing but "big, dirty, and noisy." Actually, she liked it. The place was alive and seemed friendly enough. She laughed to herself as she walked through Times Square and saw a sign that said: "Company's coming—let's clean up!"

Times Square was a long way from Martinsville, Georgia, where Mrs. Woodruff was born, the granddaughter of a slave. Her family moved "North"—to Winston-Salem, North Carolina—and she began working at 14, became a mother at 17, and began raising hell in her early 20s. Most of her fighting was for her kids, which meant she was "making trouble" about schools. After Winston-Salem schools were integrated in 1955, black parents and children believed it was important to have one of their own as Reynolds High School's Homecoming Queen. She helped devise the strategy: put three black girls up against the three white candidates, but quietly pass the word to black students to vote for a particular girl, who would then be a sure winner against the divided white vote. A political natural, she served as a local Model Cities commissioner and was a member of the executive board of the Forsyth County Democratic Organization. Mrs. Woodruff's choice for president in 1976 had been Hubert Humphrey—"He fought with black folks, and I love him"—but since September, 1975, she had been very interested in Jimmy Carter after checking him out with friends in Georgia. By the time she met the Georgian in March, she was determined to get to New York to vote for "this good man who wasn't part of the Washington gang." Her first chance to become a delegate, under North Carolina's complicated selection rules, came at the Fifth Congressional District Convention on May 8 in Sparta. Because of Carter's victory margin over George Wallace in the state's March 23 primary election, the caucus was charged with selecting four delegates—

three for Carter and one for Wallace—and three alternates
to the Democratic National Convention from lists approved
by the Carter and Wallace campaign staffs.

There was a simplicity about Mazie Woodruff, but she
was anything but naive. At Sparta, she was part of a loose
—and secret—coalition with two white candidates, Ken
Babb, a young Winston-Salem lawyer, and Cecil Porter
of Wilkes County, one of the rural areas in the Fifth District.
As long as they kept it quiet, the three of them, with very
different friends, might be able to collect enough votes to
get them all to New York. The idea seemed fine until Babb
and Porter saw the official ballot, a single typed sheet—
their names were at the bottom of a list of a dozen Carter-
approved candidates.

There are no sure rules in politics, but one of the surest
is this: Names at the top of a complicated ballot get more
votes than names at the bottom. "Cecil," Babb said, "we've
got to reverse the order of these names. You give them all
the opportunity in the world to vote against you if you're
last on the list. They get down to the end and they don't
have a vote left for you even if they want to." Babb and
Porter went to District Chairman Clarence Carter and
volunteered to Xerox the list for the first day's balloting.
Then they retyped the list in reverse order with their own
names on top—Mazie Woodruff's, though, was still in the
middle.

The first three names did win in the district caucus, with
Babb first, Porter second, and a relatively unknown candidate named "Rebel" Haynes, who was listed third on the
new ballot, finishing third. Fourth and fifth were Mazie
Woodruff and James Sheppard, a young assistant to the
district's popular congressman, Stephen Neal. She and Sheppard were immediately offered alternate spots.

No! Mrs. Woodruff walked to the front of the old
Alleghany County Courthouse, telling the 200 Democrats

there that the times had changed, that they were not going to send three white men as delegates and have her sit in the alternate section in the grandstand seats of Madison Square Garden. "I came here today just like you, looking for a piece of the loaf," she said. "I am not going to settle for crumbs. I won't go as an alternate. I won't go to New York and watch other people vote for president. *I won't sit in the balcony!* For too long my people have sat in the balcony."

Within a week, most North Carolinians had seen those words in their newspapers. Mazie Woodruff had no trouble at all being elected one of the 15 at-large delegates chosen by the Democratic State Convention on June 12. Now she was walking down Broadway, determined to get her seat on the floor of the Garden early, to hear every word of every session and tell her 13 grandchildren about it.

Except for a bite of apple for Cleveland's Channel 3, Clare Smith hadn't eaten all day, and there was no time if she was going to catch the 6:30 P.M. Ohio delegation's bus to Madison Square Garden. Being famous takes a lot of time, and Clare had already done more than 50 interviews at home and in New York. Like Lillian Carter, the Candidate's Mother, or Fritz Efaw, the Draft Dodger, the Youngest Delegate had become a professional. She knew her part, and she knew what questions she would be asked. Her answers quickly became automatic, compact, suitably girlish, and offered appropriate thanks to her parents.

Youngest Delegate, how did you get here when you aren't old enough to vote?

"In Ohio and a few other states, if a person's eighteenth birthday is on or before Election Day on November 2, he or she can register to vote, run for an office like delegate, and vote in the state's primary election. My birthday happens to be October 14."

Well, Youngest Delegate, how did you get started?

"Last November in a government class at school, I saw the film *The Making of the President, 1972.* I saw the Convention scenes and had the passing thought that it would be exciting to be a delegate. I had been doing stuff in the Carter campaign for quite a while. Right before the district caucuses to select Carter delegates on March 11, my father found out that very few women were running, and he urged me and my friend, Beth Farnsworth, who's eighteen, to run. I forget what we said in our speeches. Everyone else was saying that they were state representatives or city councilmen and here we were, two high school kids. We were placed on the slate of thirty-eight at-large Carter delegates, who all won. Beth finished ninth, and I tied for seventeenth—she has blonde hair, and I don't."

Is there anything special you want to do in New York, Youngest Delegate?

"I want to meet Hunter Thompson."

Eugene McCarthy, a Democratic vice-presidential possibility in 1964 and the antiwar candidate of 1968, was no longer part of all this. He had given up his Senate seat from Minnesota and the Democratic party, too—declaring himself an independent candidate for president. He was in New York because that's where the television cameras and the money were—he gave interviews and looked for help to finance his efforts to get his third-party candidacy on the ballot in as many states as possible, a formidable undertaking because most state election laws were written by Democratic and Republican legislatures interested in preserving the two-party monopoly in elective office.

Before the first Convention session, McCarthy went to Pietro's Restaurant on East 45th Street to try to persuade three of his richest 1968 and 1972 backers to try with him once again. Howard Stein, Martin Peretz, and Martin Fife were having none of it—all they were having was dinner before going down to the Garden. And they were almost finished with that when McCarthy walked in. He said that was all right, he did not want a whole meal, and he began eating what was left on their plates.

"This is great," Marty Fife laughed. "Jimmy Carter is eating caviar, and you're eating table scraps."

"I'll tell you, I can beat him," McCarthy said. "A man who sells peanuts can't think big enough to be president."

When Fife and the others left, McCarthy was going from table to table, shaking hands.

The Time Inc. cocktail party—"By Invitation Only. 5:30 P.M. to 7:30 P.M.," the official Convention schedule said—was *the* place to be seen, heard, and photographed before the first session began. Senator Hubert Humphrey, the former vice-president and the party's nominee in 1968, balanced a huge roast beef sandwich and water glass filled with scotch at one of the two bars in the penthouse of the weekly newsmagazine's Sixth Avenue tower. He put both down when he saw Pat Brown, the 71-year-old former California governor and the father of the state's current one. The two men had avoided each other, barely spoken for four years, since Brown had endorsed George McGovern against Humphrey in the 1972 California presidential primary.

"Pat!" Humphrey said, embracing the smaller man. "Pat! The Humphreys and the Browns really blew it. This all could have been a different story." Now they were allies again because Pat's son, Jerry, had almost stopped the other outsider, Jimmy Carter—a blockage that could have deadlocked the Convention and led to the nomination of Humphrey, who had run for president every year since 1960, except for 1964, when he ran for vice-president.

At the other bar, another generational figure was holding

court. Tom Hayden, 37, who had been tried on federal conspiracy charges as a leader of the demonstrations against the Chicago Convention that nominated Humphrey in 1968, was talking about his recent—and unsuccessful— race for the Democratic nomination for U.S. senator in California. "Look, man," said Hayden, looking over a reporter's shoulder, "I'm just too busy to talk now. If you want to know what my ideas are, why don't you go read my article in the *New York Times*."

Someone introduced Hayden to Peter Kaplan, a 22-year-old editor of the *Harvard Crimson*. "I'm sorry, I didn't get your name," said Kaplan, a young man who always looked as if he had just lost something terribly important. "Why don't you just go on to wherever you're going," Hayden said, pushing Kaplan along and turning to a *Time* editor.

The party was breaking up, and the people there— senators, ambassadors, publishers, editors, and columnists —told one another that they would get together after the session at that night's *Rolling Stone* party. That would be the place to be then, so much so that Dick Tuck's *Reliable Source* had printed a copy of the R.S.V.P. invitation for those not important enough to have gotten one, two weeks before.

Bob Strauss was one of the professionals who had thought —as Humphrey had hoped—that the Convention would be deadlocked, that perhaps six candidates would come to New York with sizable blocs of delegates but that no one would have anywhere near the 1,505 votes needed for the nomination. That seemed to be the logical, predictable result of the democratization of the party's delegate selection and the proliferation of primary elections and precinct caucuses.

Knowing that control over procedure more often than not translates into control over events, the chairman began formulating a plan—in personal memos he began dictating in November, 1975—to break such a deadlock. "A smoke-filled room with everyone invited in" was his description in one of those memos.

A group of about 50 Democratic leaders representing visible constituencies—organized labor, women, and blacks among them—would have met to recommend a ticket, or optional tickets, to the Convention. Their deliberations, Strauss figured, would have to be televised to give them the legitimacy he wanted. *But* the caucus of 50 would have acted only on options prepared by a smaller group of 12 —a group that, if recent party history were a guide, Strauss would have controlled. Members of the smaller group listed in Strauss's memos included: James Rowe, a Strauss adviser and Washington attorney whose party credentials went back to service with Franklin Roosevelt; Joseph Duffey, a liberal activist; Governors Reubin Askew of Florida and Raul Castro of Arizona; Senators Robert Byrd of West Virginia and Abraham Ribicoff of Connecticut; House Majority Leader Thomas ("Tip") O'Neill of Massachusetts; and Representative Yvonne Burke of California. The deadlock plan had gone far enough that letters calling a meeting of the smaller group had been written, but never sent, in April. About that time, Strauss joked that a group like that might turn to him as the nominee for vice-president—anyway, he said it was a joke.

The deadlock procedure—options-recommendations-action—was a model for the techniques that the chairman had used to gain control of the party and to produce the Convention he wanted, a unity show for television. Dullness was in the eye of the beholder. Again and again, Strauss had channeled party business through a maze of bodies he had appointed—he created 13 commissions, councils, and committees in three years—establishing the options-recommendations-action pattern. In the end, the actual decision-making body—in this case, the Convention it-self—had almost no options. The key decision controlling the Convention had been made on October 14, 1975, at a meeting of the full Democratic National Committee, two members from each state, part-timers flown into Wash-ington for one day to consider recommendations by the Executive Committee, a body wholly controlled by Strauss. The DNC that day approved the recommendation that minority reports of any Convention committee had to be signed by 25 percent of the committee's *total* membership, instead of by only 10 percent of the members *present*— and those minority reports had to be filed within 24 hours of a decision. If the delegates to the Convention did not like the majority reports on rules, credentials, or the party platform, they would have to suspend the rules by a two-thirds vote of *all* delegates, not just those present and voting.

The delegates had not realized it yet, but they were just about prisoners of two Roberts—Rules of Order and Strauss. "I decided the day I became chairman that I would pay any price for a 25 percent rule," Strauss said. "I wasn't interested in having every little sliver of opinion presented on prime-time television. At 10 percent, the gays and the abortion people and other weirdos could get together and sign each other's petitions—'You sign ours, and we'll sign yours.' We cured the platform problems and Carter cured the rest."

Andy Shea was Strauss's Convention manager—"one of the finest young men I've ever known," the chairman said; "he's not in business for himself"—and the Convention manager was traditionally the first speaker of the first night.* It was a nonevent as far as television was concerned. Jackie Gleason and Julie Andrews were cavorting in a

* Shea was paid $90,000 for his year's labor—plus expenses, including a $1,150-a-month apartment on Central Park South.

musical rerun on ABC; Rosalynn Carter was on CBS saying that she believed her 8-year-old daughter, Amy, could have a normal childhood; and John Chancellor and David Brinkley were talking about Italian food on NBC. Amy's father had had Italian food that night at Mamma Leone's on West 48th Street, a restaurant favored by tourists. The Carter family menu—veal piccata—was transmitted to the networks by Alan Fein, a 21-year-old volunteer from Jacksonville, Florida, who had come to New York the week before and talked his way into running a Xerox machine in the press office. Within two days, he was in an office outside the candidate's 21st-floor suite—"They told me everybody needs lackeys and that's the way to get close to the big shots"—telling Theodore H. White and other people he had read about that he was sorry, but they couldn't come up. Fein watched Chancellor repeat the menu he had just dictated to an NBC lackey and said, "So that's the way it works."

Shea finished his opening remarks and went behind the podium. His 10-year-old son, Andy, came down from the VIP section and said: "Daddy, what did you say? We couldn't hear you out there."

Shea's son wasn't the only one. The worst place to hear the Convention was inside Madison Square Garden. The argument over whose fault that was—and whether the sound system was being deliberately sabotaged—had become so bitter that both the Secret Service and Manhattan homicide detectives were patrolling the ceiling of the Garden and investigating improbable accidents.

The cops and the Secret Service were called in on July 6 by Garden officials when a safety-locked 4½-pound television bulb dropped 75 feet from the ceiling to the floor where network technicians were working. An investigating team sent into the dim space above the suspended ceiling by the Pool—the joint camera, lighting, and sound operation of the three networks—discovered that more than 100 of the 425 Maxi-Brute bulbs put into the ceiling for the Convention were loose, or loosened. The 1,000-watt bulbs had last been checked—and found safety-locked —just before the Fourth of July holiday.

Installation of the Maxi-Brutes and operation of the sound system were two points of contention in a vocal running battle involving executives and unions of the Garden and the networks. The fight was over jurisdiction— which meant work and money to the competing unions and control to the executives. There had been months of negotiation, shouting, harassment, and sabotage as Local 3 of the International Brotherhood of Electrical Workers, the Garden's union, and the International Alliance of Theatrical and Stage Employees and the National Association of Broadcast Employees and Technicians, the networks' unions, struggled for lighting and sound supremacy.*

Network executives complained bitterly about the IBEW's demands for "standby electricians" on all electrical work done in the building—CBS budgeted $30,000 for standbys and the Pool budgeted $20,000—claiming that it was a "legal shakedown," that the extra men were not necessary. Mickey McCauley, the Garden's executive vice-

---

* The struggle between house and network unions is an old one that surfaces almost every time public events are televised, especially in Madison Square Garden, which has just about the strongest union structure of any arena in the country. It also has one of the worst reputations for graft. In interviews for this book, television producers and rock-concert promoters said that they had paid off in the past to cover or stage events in the Garden—but those producers and promoters asked for anonymity, saying they would have to work in the arena again. The going price to "turn on the lights" to televise basketball, hockey, or music, according to the producers, was $5,000. During the pre-Convention period, executives of two television networks said they "tipped" Garden employees to turn on the lights for work or for tours of corporate VIPs or advertisers—the tip, they said, was $50 in cash added to the normal billing for the service.

president and Convention coordinator, was not worried about the legal stuff, but called together Convention contractors, suppliers, and network executives to tell them: "I just told my people that any man with his hand out is out of a job. No payoffs—I don't care if that closes this building forever. Now I'm telling you that if I hear you're paying off, if any of my people are offered money, you're out. I'll throw you out of this building. If anyone asks, report it to me."

The television Pool then had its own meeting and decided to resist all demands to pay for IBEW standby electricians. But the Pool managers—most of them from NBC —also held meetings to discuss how to deal with sabotage, worrying most about cut cables. After a series of tense confrontations between Steve Alper, the Pool's unit manager, and Norman Leonard, who was both the Garden's chief electrician and a power within the IBEW, the Pool surreptitiously laid an auxiliary sound cable system to bypass the control boards of the Garden's public-address system, which was controlled by Leonard—just in case.

The first investigation of the loosened Maxi-Brutes by Manhattan Homicide was inconclusive. Detective Sergeant James Porter reported that the falling bulb was the result of "human failure"—which could have meant anything. The Pool decided to pay to put safety screens under the 425 extra bulbs needed for television cameras. The Police Department assigned Sergeant Porter to head a three-man team to stay through the Convention to act as a buffer between the Pool and the IBEW, while Secret Service agents were assigned to 24-hour patrol of the walkspace above the ceiling. The Garden was an armed camp long before bodyguards arrived with presidential candidates and assorted other important folks arrived with their bodyguards.

Just before 9:30, Edward Bennett Williams, the country's highest-paid defense attorney and the president of the Washington Redskins football team, came to the podium to give his report as treasurer of the Democratic National Committee. NBC used the time to formally introduce its four floor correspondents: Tom Brokaw, Tom Pettit, Cassie Mackin, and John Hart. On CBS, floorperson Lesley Stahl was interviewing Representative Bella Abzug of New York and called her "Bella"—Ms. Stahl's earphones crackled with the voice of floor producer Don Hewitt saying, "At CBS we do *not* use first names." Williams, a man used to being called "Mister" and being listened to, came off the podium after the delegates had almost universally ignored him—he did not know that most of them could not hear him—and told the first person he met, "That was the most humiliating experience of my life."

Williams was calmer than his 1972 counterpart. When the previous financial report was ignored by television, the treasurer came off the podium at Miami Beach and demanded that the Convention manager, Richard Murphy, immediately fire the DNC's television adviser. "Calm down, Bob, we're not firing anyone," Murphy said to Robert Strauss.

The Floor Game had begun. An uncalculated amount of energy, probably about enough to heat Denver for a year, is expended at any convention to get on the floor. People who don't have to be there, *have* to be there. One of the first players was Diane von Furstenberg, the country's most famous dress designer, who happened to make her move under the acerbic gaze of Jane O'Reilly, a *Washington Star* columnist recording the occasion in her personal journal: "Diane von Furstenberg, in brown and white von Furstenberg, wearing an NBC badge and 'Honored Guest' tag, . . . made several sorties onto the floor, or rather at the floor—pointing to luminaries below, but held back by stalwart guards for lack of a 'Floor' pass. I had just completed a rude remark about her to Al Lowenstein when she passed behind me and Al nearly knocked me down in an effort to extend affectionate greetings. She huddled in the manner of her Central European ancestors, clutching her elbows and looking slightly exhausted by the load she bears. But, my God, the Convention was, in effect, dressed by her —at $80 to $100 a throw."

Joe Kaselak, wearing the same "Honored Guest" pass, in this case Mrs. Vanik's, was having the same trouble. Pacing outside Gate 5, he was convinced that he was not going to make it when David Strand, a Cleveland councilman, came by, asking, "How ya doing, Joe?"

"Miserable, I can't get on the floor."

"I'm tired, take mine," Strand said, slipping the elastic string with the blue "Delegate" credential over his head. Kaselak moved as quickly as he could to the center of the floor, looking into the rafters for network camera locations. He spotted an ABC camera moving toward a tall reporter, a woman, lining up two delegates in the South Dakota section. It wasn't NBC, but what the hell, Kaselak maneuvered himself behind the delegates, a man and a woman, who turned out to be husband and wife delegates, Henry and Ellie Decker of Pierre.

The ABC correspondent, who unknowingly hosted Kaselak's 1976 debut, was Ann Compton. At 29, she was the youngest network reporter on the floor—and the least experienced. Four years before, she had paid her own way to the Democratic and Republican conventions to do free-lance work for WDBJ-TV in Roanoke, Virginia. "I'm one of ABC's pet projects," she said, the network's only woman political reporter and, after only three years, their White House correspondent, earning between $1,000 and $1,500 a week, depending on how often she appeared on the seven o'clock news. She had not taken a day off in six weeks, but considered the Convention a piece of cake—"the dress rehearsal for the Republicans"—flipping through Norman Mailer's *Some Honorable Men* for the feel of floor action and having her makeup done at Cinandre's on East 57th Street. "I seem to be incapable of developing butterflies," she had told a friend.

On Sunday, the day of ABC's pre-Convention show, Ann Compton woke up with a mouth full of canker sores. Nerves, a doctor told her.

While Edward Bennett Williams was speaking, Tom Murray, the usher behind the podium, looked down the cinderblock corridors where sweating basketball players usually walked to work and said to himself, "Oh, shit!"

"I'm sorry, but I can't let you through here with those credentials," were his next words.

"But I'm the lieutenant governor of New York," said Mary Anne Krupsak.

Murray knew that, and he spoke quickly: "If I don't stop you here, they're just going to do it on the podium, and I'll get screwed for letting you through."

Ms. Krupsak smiled at that and went looking for a pass. She came back, ticketed correctly, and went up the podium stairs for a five-minute speech—another perfect opportunity for the networks to cut away for commercials or commentary. But CBS and NBC did not cut away, because Ms. Krupsak had a sign-language interpreter with her— Oscar Cohen of the Lexington School for the Deaf—and both networks stayed on her, using an inset of the sign translation. Good television. Good politics.

Warren Beatty, the best-looking of the good-looking California delegation, spent a good part of opening night hanging around Jimmy Carter's Trailer Camp. The actor signed autographs until the television lights came on; as each of the three networks showed Carter's Garden command center—three guarded office-trailers just off the convention floor—Beatty would grab the nearest available Carter aide and begin nodding and pointing in earnest conversation. On screen, Beatty looked like a convincing political strategist even when he was talking about the weather or asking for directions to the nearest men's room.

Behind a green and white sign that read "Carter Country—Population 1505+", the three rented trailers were arranged in a sort of Y-formation with a VIP trailer, set up as a living room, forming the tail. The arms of arrangement were a 30-foot long press trailer where reporters lined up for interviews and tours, and a 40-foot long delegate-communications trailer. The longer trailer, actually two of the aluminum boxes linked together, was where the action was. Inside, Rick Hutcheson, Hamilton Jordan's deputy campaign manager, commanded his small staff of delegate counters and their tools—charts and blackboards listing Carter delegate strength, telephones to floor captains and delegation leaders, and hot-line phones to the candidate and Jordan back at the Americana.

What the plans for the command trailer had also included was a padlocked "private section," an espionage room where radio technicians could electronically eavesdrop on the communications of other candidates and the television networks. For months, the Carter staff had weighed the advantages of spying against the risks of being trapped in their own Watergate—and had decided to take the chance.

Planning for the "private section" had begun in April between Hutcheson's assistant, William Simon; the Carter convention co-ordinator, James Gammill; and an electrical engineering researcher at Georgia Institute of Technology named Ronald Pearl. Hutcheson and Gammill were convinced—"We were paranoid about dirty tricks being played on us," the convention co-ordinator said—that other candidates would attempt to sabotage their telephone system inside Madison Square Garden, and they asked Pearl to develop a back-up communications system. But they got—and approved—much more than that.

Like many of Carter's most important assistants, Hutcheson and Gammill were in their early 20's and had no experience in national politics. Gammill, who was just graduating from high school in 1972 when the Democrats last convened, had learned about conventions by talking to older hands and by reading. What had most impressed him was Hunter Thompson's *Fear and Loathing on the Campaign Trail '72*—especially a few pages in which Rick Stearns, George McGovern's command trailer chief, said things like: "A guy with an axe could have demolished that communications system in thirty seconds . . . They wouldn't have hesitated if they'd had the chance." When Gammill talked to Stearns to find out who "they" were, he was told the people around Hubert Humphrey and Scoop Jackson.

So, Ron Pearl came back to the Carter campaign with a system, costing more than $30,000, of walkie-talkies and a base radio station that included Ultra High Frequency (UHF) scanning equipment—and a plan to use it to intercept all in-air communications inside the Garden. The "private section" in the trailer would have monitored all radio communications between opposing candidates and their floor leaders, and instructions from network producers to their correspondents. Among other things, the Carter staff assumed that the networks would be tapping their telephones—and by the end of the Convention, Jim Gammill would be convinced that the assumption was true.*

* Officials of all three networks denied that they used electronic or telephone surveillance, although they added that they could not guarantee that the techniques had not been used sometime in the past. In 1968,

The electronic equipment for the Carter system was ordered by Pearl in May, but the lease agreement for walkie-talkies was put on "reserve hold" on June 10, after Jimmy Carter won the Ohio primary and it appeared that he would have no serious opposition in New York. "The nomination was locked up by then," Gammill said, "and the back-up system just didn't seem cost-effective."

The eavesdropping plan, however, was still alive—the reasoning was that if the Carter command trailer knew in advance what CBS, NBC and ABC were planning, campaign aides could be sent to story locations and perhaps have a hand in determining what news would be seen during the Convention. On July 6, six days before the Convention began, Simon and Pearl flew from Atlanta to New York to decide where Pearl's equipment and technicians could be located—hidden, really. Gammill, Carter television advisor Barry Jagoda and William White, who handled Carter arrangements inside the Garden, gave Simon and Pearl a tour of the hall and trailers.

Simon, Gammill and Pearl, though, kept pulling away from the other two and whispering among themselves. Overhearing them talking about keeping reporters far from "communications gear," Jagoda asked, "What the hell's going on here?"

When he found out, Jagoda, a former CBS convention producer, began shouting: "You must be crazy. Didn't you ever hear of Watergate? If somebody finds out, it'll destroy Carter!"

For two hours, Jagoda and White, who both happened to

---

an NBC assistant director, Enid Roth, pleaded *nolo contendere* to federal charges that she placed a listening device inside a closed meeting of the DNC's Platform Committee during the Chicago convention. She was fined $1,000 in United States District Court and was suspended by the network. In New York in 1976, Ms. Roth was the director of NBC's coverage.

be in their late 30's, argued against the plan. "You're talking about bugging," Jagoda said during lunch at Harry
M's, a bar on the Garden's ground level. "Do you understand that? I've heard of people not understanding the past
—you don't seem to understand the present!

"Does Jordan know about this? Does Jimmy?" Jagoda
finally asked. "Kill it, or I'm calling Hamilton right now!"

"Okay," Gammill said. "We must have been crazy."

Mark Gasarch, the lawyer who had volunteered to be a
Convention aide, had ended up with the title "chief," security credential 1041, walkie-talkie unit 20, and was in
command of 72 aides and 11 aide-supervisors. Being no
fool, he stationed himself at the entrance to Sections 56,
57, and 58 of the Garden's Lower Promenade, directly
under the CBS anchor booth. That was the most exclusive
VIP section, divided by an aisle into the "Bride's side" and
the "Groom's side"—the side controlled by Bob Strauss and
the side controlled by Jimmy Carter. If Gasarch was going
to make new friends during the Convention, they might as
well be Carters, Strausses, Kennedys, and such.

VVIP—Very Very Important Person—admission was by
"Honored Guest" credential and a 3-by-5-inch card that
had to be presented to Gasarch or one of his assistants. But
the section was not filled the first night, and Chief Gasarch
was sure he knew why: "It's the New York style—the 'in'
thing was not to be at the Convention, necessarily, but to
have a ticket for it, or, and this was the real 'in' thing, to
know there was a ticket available for you if you wanted it,
which you didn't."

One of the first friends Gasarch made was Helen Strauss,
the chairman's wife. She asked him why, if these were the
best seats in the house, she couldn't hear what was being
said on the podium. "Unit 20 to Base. Mrs. Strauss is having trouble hearing," he said into his walkie-talkie. "Could

you contact the podium?" Within 20 seconds, Gasarch saw Cliff Cassidy, the chairman of the DNC Security Advisory Committee, dispatching assistants on the podium, one to push the speaker closer to the microphone, another to check what was happening with Norman Leonard and his Garden electricians—then Cassidy threw a quick salute toward Mrs. Strauss across the arena.

Across the aisle from Mrs. Strauss, Lesley Stahl of CBS was leaning into the section and interviewing 8-year-old Amy Carter, the candidate's daughter.

"Do you have any advice for the young people of America?"

"No."

"Thank you, Amy. Back to you, Walter."

The first blocks of the Convention schedule had been filled in in October, nine months before the event—and the very first one penciled in by Chairman Strauss had been: "11:00 P.M., Monday. Keynote—Barbara Jordan (20 minutes)."

On one level, it was revenge. Strauss resented what he felt was three years of harassment from vocal black and feminist leaders as he tried to build a unified, ordered, and solvent Democratic party. *They* were not going to get the podium and television at *his* Convention. They might not like Barbara Jordan—in fact, they didn't—but there was no way they could open their mouths in public about it. Ms. Jordan, 40, U.S. Representative from Houston, Texas, was visibly black and female, so much so that she was constantly being used as a symbol that America worked—if a very large black woman who looked, to many Americans, like a maid, could become a national leader, well . . . But Ms. Jordan felt no obligation to narrow her base to movements. She had been a protégé of Lyndon Johnson and she spoke Bob Strauss's language: "I'm neither a black politician nor a woman politician. Just a politician. A professional politician."

On another level, it was inspiration. Strauss had picked the most electrifying speaker in his party. With a deep, rolling voice, indefinable accent, and the cadence of her Baptist-preacher father, Ms. Jordan had become a national figure in 1974 with one powerful statement at the House Judiciary Committee hearings on the possible impeachment of President Richard Nixon: " 'We, the people'—I felt for many years that somehow George Washington and Alexander Hamilton just left me out by mistake. But through the process of amendment, interpretation, and court decision, I have finally been included in 'We, the people.' . . . My faith in the Constitution is whole, it is complete, it is total."

Strauss had teamed Ms. Jordan with John Glenn, the All-American. Marine hero, first American to orbit the earth, and now a U.S. senator from Ohio, one who had earned some respect in Washington because he did not live by press release alone—John Glenn was on the downside of the fame curve, and it gave him a certain sense of perspective lacking in most politicians. He had worked on his speech for three months—checking out copies of every keynote address for the past 100 years from the Library of Congress—searching for thoughtful, dignified directions. The speech *was* dignified. And it was a disaster. Glenn was not helped by the fuzzy sound system, which his staff later blamed for his obvious failure, and the noise level on the floor kept rising until he was as alone as he had been in space when he closed with lines like: "We must select new leaders, leaders with vision, leaders who will set a different tone for this nation, a tone of opportunities sought and seized, a tone of national purpose."

Even Strauss was not listening; he was pacing back and forth behind the podium, telling Barbara Jordan—five times—not to be nervous. "Barbara," he said, "there'll be no one out in the hall listening to you. Forget them. Let them talk to each other. You're talking to millions of people on television."

As the congresswoman was being helped up the stairs— her walking was restricted by calcium deposits on one knee —Strauss said, "Honey, I've bet every chip I've got on you."

She turned back and said, "I won't let you down."

She didn't. "There is something different and special about this opening night," she began. "I am a keynote speaker. . . . The past notwithstanding, a Barbara Jordan is before you tonight. This is one additional bit of evidence that the American Dream need not forever be deferred."

The delegates and guests, for the first time, were quiet. In the NBC anchor booth, spotter Mark Shields said: "They'll go nuts. Barbara Jordan is a symbol, and she could read the Manhattan phone book to these people and they'd applaud."

Across the street in the Penn Bar of the Statler Hilton, men and women began clustering around the television set, then demanded that Randy Taylor and his band stop playing until Ms. Jordan finished saying her piece. She did that by quoting Abraham Lincoln: "As I would not be a slave, so I would not be a master. This expresses my idea of Democracy. Whatever differs from this, to the extent of the difference is no Democracy."

"Oh, Gordon," said Bob Strauss to his friend and assistant Gordon Wynne, "we just knocked one out of the goddamned ballpark."

By the end of the session, Joe Kaselak had gotten his face into television cameras twice more. One of those times, he had spotted ABC's Frank Reynolds interviewing Howard Metzenbaum, the Democratic candidate for the U.S. Senate in Ohio, while Metzenbaum's daughter, Suzie, stood aside out of camera range—Kaselak took Suzie's arm and moved in behind her father.

After the final gavel, he looked, as he always did, for NBC's four floor correspondents—Brokaw, Pettit, Hart, and Mackin—to settle into delegate chairs for their nightly post-Convention chat with anchormen Chancellor and Brinkley. He sat a row behind them, trying to look like a fifth horseman, until someone in the control room noticed him and sent down three men. "Hey you," one of them said when the cameras shifted away from the floor, "get outta there!"

Kaselak got even by finding Daniel Troy, a 28-year-old councilman from the Cleveland suburb of Willowick. "Dan," he called, "wanna get on television? Here's what you do. Walk ten steps toward that aisle seat by the NBC reporters. Set down your briefcase and, as you do, look to your right. Your face will be on camera." Troy did it and came back grinning. "Now," Kaselak said, "go back and pick it up, looking to your right the same way and you'll be on again."

When the session ended at 11:28 P.M.—two minutes ahead of schedule, as Bob Strauss happily pointed out again and again behind the podium—the public relations departments of the three networks began their nightly ritual of printing press releases on their journalistic triumphs. ABC's *News Briefs* reported that their special guest commentator, Senator Barry Goldwater, the 1964 Republican nominee for President, had noted: "I am not convinced that there's unity in the Democratic party, even though we saw a good show tonight. I just cannot bring myself to believe that the North is ever going to allow a southerner in this day and age to head the Democratic party."

Another item reported: "Nearly two-thirds of a mile of grade-B chain, in three-foot segments, has been distributed to ABC News personnel and guests at the Democratic National Convention. The small segments of chain adorn the neck of the wearer and hold identification cards and various credentials that provide access in and around Madison Square Garden. That much chain has exhausted the supply of three local New York hardware stores. Reports from the ABC News supply room indicate that perhaps one mile or more of the chain may be used before the Convention ends."

The little party that Dick Celeste's staff had put together for John Glenn was a success, but a sad one. Walter Cronkite did come, but the guest of honor was quiet and most people there tried to avoid the obvious: Glenn's keynote speech. There were people in the room who knew that the senator, despite his public diffidence, very much wanted the vice-presidency, and there were a couple who had heard a rumor that Hamilton Jordan, Carter's manager, had reacted to Glenn's performance by saying, "I guess that eliminates one guy."

Well, at least the Ohio delegation had stood up and applauded, one man said in a corner. Then someone told him the delegation was actually standing because Warren Beatty, the actor, who was a California delegate, was pointed out as he walked by.* Cronkite was stopped by John ("Socko") Wiethe, the party chairman of Ohio's Hamilton County, who politely told him that he thought the CBS anchorman went a little too far in calling Glenn "dull," but Socko added that, in general, he thought the star was doing a hell of job.

---

* Jimmy Carter's staff was not quite as impressed with Warren Beatty as the Ohio delegates. During the Convention, the actor volunteered to set up a "Stars for Carter" committee, saying he was committed to the candidate now that Edward Kennedy, his first choice, and Jerry Brown, his second, were out of the running. "Thanks," said Gerald Rafshoon, Carter's principal media adviser, "but we don't take sloppy thirds."

At the end, Glenn came up to Celeste and said, "I just want to thank you for all this." The lieutenant governor told his staff meeting that night how pleased he was by that because he and Glenn had never really been close—and, no matter what they thought in New York, John Glenn was a very important friend to have in Ohio.

At 1:00 A.M., Jimmy Carter's New York coordinator got to the door of 49 East 68th Street, raised his hand to the policeman at the door, and said: "It's all right, I'm Bill vanden Heuvel."

"Get out of here before I lose my cool," said the cop, one of six of New York's finest holding back the first mob of the Convention. Almost everyone in the milling, cursing, laughing, confused crowd was right out of the pages of *People* magazine—Lauren Bacall, Ben Bradlee, Jane Fonda, Chevy Chase, Jean Kennedy Smith, Carl Bernstein, Paul Simon, Senator Gary Hart, Representative Bella Abzug, Warren Beatty, and, sitting elegantly on the hood of a Plymouth, Dorothy Schiff, the 73-year-old publisher of the *New York Post*.

They all held engraved invitations on ecru noteboard saying:

ROLLING STONE MAGAZINE
invites you to a supper
with
THE JIMMY CARTER CAMPAIGN STAFF

The purpose of the party, as much as anything else, was to allow the established stars of politics, journalism, and entertainment—three businesses that tend to confuse their realms—to look over the new boys, these southerners with names like Jody and Griff, and see if they were sophisticated enough to take over the country. But the beautiful street people, stepping on and wrinkling the work of Gucci and Halston, got to the townhouse too late. Early arrivals had brought friends and the house had been packed by crashers, some of them waving the phony invitations printed by Dick Tuck's *Reliable Source.* The doors were locked and guarded with the Carter folks inside and the beautiful ones outside. Patrick Anderson, a novelist and sometime journalist, who was writing and rewriting Carter's acceptance speech, came out, looked at the scene, and said: "My God, it's *Day of the Locust!*"

Bill vanden Heuvel and a lot of the people on East 68th Street wondered whether the Carter first team, the southerners, were ever going to let anyone in. Earlier in the night, 15 blocks away at one of the Old Order's places, the "21" Club, Barbara Walters, biding her time until she took over as anchorwoman on the ABC Nightly News, had run into Gerald Rafshoon, Carter's Atlanta-based media adviser.

"We won because we understood the mood of the country," said Rafshoon, one of the Carter people who refused to wear a tie, even at "21." "There are five of us running this campaign. We're the same five who are going to run things after the nomination. Who are these people here tonight? Punch Sulzberger? Ben Bradlee? Dorothy Schiff? Where? Walter Cronkite? Sure they're important. But they don't make an election. How do I feel about all these people in one room? Let's just say I'm 'whelmed.' "

The Carter folks loved to talk that way. Part of the energy core of their campaign was a kind of personal populism, the bundled resentments of outsiders; they had the wrong accents, went to the wrong schools, had the wrong friends, got the wrong jobs. Now they were sure they were going to take over that world that always seemed peopled exclusively by former editors of the *Harvard Crimson* and the *Yale Law Review,* where everybody had been some-body's roommate or had clerked for a Supreme Court justice.

Big talk. But Washington was a very seductive place, and being part of it all had turned older heads than Jerry Raf-shoon's. "I'll make you a bet," said Clay Felker, the editor of *New York* magazine, who started out in Webster Groves, Missouri. "If they get to Washington, they'll wear ties like everybody else. Rafshoon, too."

Rafshoon and the rest, however, had not taken over the country yet—and they hardly seemed immune from the charms of power and the fruits of victory. He met Barbara Howar, a Washington author with a reputation for being where the action was, at the Convention and, after they quickly became a Georgetown couple, a friend said, "Well, Jerry, let's hope Carter wins in November."

Annie, the little crook from Dorchester, Mass., was not a Delancey Street whore. Her usual style was to work up-town hotels, helping a sucker undress to find his wallet—and, with luck, lifting it. She preferred out-of-towners be-cause they were usually neater, folding their pants and jackets over a chair which she tried to place within reach of the bed. They also seemed to have a highly developed fear of cockroaches. If they tried to hang their clothes in the closet, she started talking about roaches, telling them that once they got in a suit, you could never get them out.

But by midnight, aggressive cops on Broadway and Park Avenue had driven Annie downtown to Delancey and Christie Streets on the Lower East Side—the "Meat Rack." By then on most nights, hundreds of prostitutes, many in their 50s, walked slowly back and forth, occasionally vary-ing the routine to go around the block. Lines of cars crept along the street most of the night—"car tricks" for $10 or

$20 were the staple of the local economy. She did $50 the whole night—two quick tricks at the New Delancey Hotel.

Uptown at a place on East 53rd Street called the Bottomless Pit, the barmaid, Mary Ault, was arguing with a man wearing a green "Carter" button. He said he was a delegate from North Dakota, a big man at home, and he wanted a discount on his drink "in the public interest."

"Forget it," she said.

"What would you say if Jimmy Carter walked in here?"

"I'd tell him the truth," Mary said, "that I hate him."

There were only three people at the Convention worth talking about, she said, George Wallace—"he'd straighten things out"—and her two favorite writers, Jimmy Breslin and Hunter Thompson. "What I'd really like out of this thing is to meet Hunter Thompson. I'd die to meet Hunter Thompson."

"Welcome, Democratic Convention Delegates" said the least picturesque sign outside the Bottomless Pit, where Mary Ault was often the only woman with any clothes on. "The Girls Come All the Way to Go All the Way," according to the motto over the door. Not quite. The layout of the place was not all that different from a miniature Madison Square Garden, but instead of the podium as the focus of attention there was a stage inside a long oval bar—and instead of politicians there were "dancers" swaying and writhing on the platform. Each dancer, young and firm and sad, would approach a customer at the bar and stand over him, fondling her nipples and moaning. Then she would drop to a sitting position, throwing her head and shoulders back, finally draping her legs over the customer's shoulders and thrusting her crotch in his face. She would begin playing with herself, panting, rolling her eyes and tongue—

until the man slipped a bill into the only thing she wore, a garter around her thigh. A small beer cost $2.75. The dancers averaged $1,000 a week. Mary usually made about $600 and she expected to make more during the Convention.

On the roof of the townhouse, five stories above the locked-out crowd at the *Rolling Stone* party on East 68th Street, Fritz Efaw, the draft evader from London, was talking with Jeff Carter, the candidate's son. It was not going well.

"I'm really here to talk about amnesty," said Efaw, who had left the United States and his studies at Massachusetts Institute of Technology to escape the draft, and had eventually become president of the Union of American Exiles.

"Okay," Carter said. "But I'm not going to talk to my father. He makes up his own mind on everything."

They tried to talk about money—"I want to make a lot before I'm thirty," Jeff Carter said—but that didn't work either. In the end, they were most comfortable talking about cars like a couple of country boys—a 23-year-old from Plains, Georgia, and a 29-year-old from Stillwater, Oklahoma.

Efaw's moods were swinging from elation to confused depression. He had seen his mother for the first time in seven years, and for the first time since running he did not feel chased. On the Friday before the Convention, legal moves to extradite him immediately to Oklahoma and jail had been delayed in New York by Magistrate Simon Chrein, who had said: "This man is a delegate to the *Democratic National Convention*. He has a *responsibility*. He voluntarily came back here to face the music. I think we should allow him to go. Mr. Efaw will be released to attend the Convention on two weeks' personal recognizance bail. . . ." *

He also enjoyed most of his celebrity—constant access to television was a startling change after lonely years of trying to get attention by picketing the American Embassy in London.

But Efaw was a Marxist, and he did not like what he saw at the *Rolling Stone* party. "The New York intelligentsia and the southern power center," he said, "are getting together to rule as a coalition."

At 2:30 A.M. in the French Quarter at the Americana Hotel, James Wooten of the *New York Times,* Stanley Cloud of *Time* magazine, and a couple of other reporters were asking Hodding Carter III of the *Delta Democrat Times* of Greenville, Mississippi, how he thought Jimmy Carter had been able to win the votes of both southern rednecks and northern blacks. They could hardly hear his answers because a half-dozen Carter delegates from Georgia and Mississippi, quite drunk and quite out of place in double-knits and white patent leather shoes, were singing: "And He walks with me and He talks with me . . ."

The Quarter's hostess, Mary Bembry, a black woman dressed in satin, walked over to the noisy group and said, "Those songs make me want to cry. I love them, they remind me of home." Home, she said later, was Durham, North Carolina, where she grew up before coming to New York 12 years ago.

* Fritz Efaw was actually an alternate delegate. There were 11 men with a total of three votes in the Democrats Abroad delegation as a result of a compromise agreement ending a dispute over whether or not to accept the votes of Americans living in Israel. Three thousand Americans living outside the country had voted in a complicated three-week primary, and disagreement broke out over the validity of 648 votes cast in Israel—in the end, delegates elected both with and without the Israeli votes were credentialed in New York.

Upstairs in the same hotel Clare Smith was trying to find Hunter Thompson. The convention session itself had been something of a disappointment. She couldn't hear much or concentrate on what was being said; she had forgotten her glasses and squinted a lot; she was hungry and she had wandered around the circular halls of the Garden before finally finding a concession stand on the second level and getting a hot dog for 85 cents.

Beth Farnsworth, Cleveland Councilman Benjamin Bonanno, and a delegate named Douglas DeLisle agreed to help the Youngest Delegate find the eminent national affairs editor of *Rolling Stone,* the rock *cum* politics journal taken with reverence by a generation-and-a-half that included Clare Smith. They had heard Thompson was at the Americana and a desk clerk readily gave Clare his room number. The four of them went upstairs and when Clare went to Thompson's door, the other three took off down the hall— the whole thing had seemed like a good idea at the time, but at the time they had been in a bar. Someone answered the door and said Thompson was out—to make sure, Clare Smith popped her head in. No Hunter Thompson.

Before he took his private elevator, which cost the Democratic National Committe $4,000 for the week, up to his 17th-floor suite at the Statler Hilton, Bob Strauss kidded about something Howard K. Smith had said in closing ABC's pre-Convention show: "We'll be back to report on the fight that's not going to happen."

"They're all saying it's a dull convention," Strauss said. Then he put two of his fingers to his mouth, wet them, and rubbed them with his thumb—like a man about to count money.

☒ Tuesday

July 13

Georgia Governor George Busbee called his delegation together on the second morning of the Convention to tell them that NBC had informed him that their cameras would focus on the state's delegates during much of the night's session. "Let's make sure that as many of us are in our seats as possible so we make a good impression," said Busbee, who had succeeded Jimmy Carter in Atlanta. "We want to appear attentive and we will have more signs available than we normally would. Let's look enthusiastic. The world will be watching."

The three television networks, in effect, were coproducers of the big show. Perhaps more than equal partners—the networks were spending more than $12 million for the week in New York, while the Democratic National Committee was spending only $2.18 million, a limit established by the Federal Election Commission. Negotiations between the networks and the DNC for coverage of the event had begun two years earlier, and officials of CBS, NBC, and ABC had traveled the country with the DNC's Site Selection Committee during the eight-month process that led to the selection of New York City. And each morning of the Convention at 8:00 A.M., network producers and executives met with DNC officials and Carter representatives at the Statler Hilton to exchange their plans for the day—game plans so that politicians and cameras would be in the same places at the same times.

"We go in there saying, 'Use me,' " said Richard Wald, the president of NBC News. "But we don't want to be used too much." In fact, there was a trade-off: Television people or television considerations often dictated the arrangements of conventions, but the political parties, Democrats and Republicans, were allowed to project their candidates and messages, legitimizing themselves electronically every four years. The imprimatur of the networks was no small thing to the two-party system at a time when other American institutions seemed to be crumbling.

"We have become Election Night," Wald told 200 NBC News employees at their last pre-Convention meeting on Sunday night. "It's no longer bonfires and city halls. . . . In many ways, we help create that sense of party unity, of life, that are these conventions. . . . Insofar as we do well, it will have been done well for this country and the people of this country."

True. But it was also true that the conventions were the quadrennial testing of the network news departments—a time when careers were made and broken—and that in 1972 Dick Wald of NBC had ended the pre-Convention meeting by sending his troops out against CBS and ABC with a ringing "We're going to beat the ass off them."

"This is when the news operation literally takes over the network for a week," said Wald. "If we do well, it means a great deal for the future," the future, in this case, meaning things like network budget allocations and job security for men like Wald. It was about the only time that news was not third in television, a business that Edward

R. Murrow of CBS once described as "an incompatible combination of show business, advertising, and news."

Conventions were where television news grew up and showed off. In 1952, the real beginning of gavel-to-gavel coverage, the industry used the Democratic and Republican get-togethers to introduce the coast-to-coast networks, linked for the first time by coaxial cables, at a time when there were only 25 million potential viewers in the country. Huntley-Brinkley, the first anchor team, was introduced in 1956; Creepie-Peepie portable cameras debuted in 1964; color was promoted coast-to-coast in 1968. The idea was to sell television sets, and sales had surged significantly before the conventions in those years. Now the market was saturated and convention coverage was actually in decline. In 1968, when ABC abandoned gavel-to-gavel coverage, CBS had 51 of its own cameras covering the Democratic National Convention in Chicago. It had 30 in Miami Beach in 1972, and only 24 in New York this time.

CBS held a "story line" meeting of correspondents and producers two hours before each session in New York. Richard Salant, the president of CBS News, and Convention producer Russ Bensley programmed their correspondents to string together interviews to answer prearranged questions like—What is the "New South"? What happened to city bosses? New York's image? Are "The Women" unhappy? Is there really unity here? One of the questions for the second session was: Are conventions really necessary?

The question may not have been academic. Conventions may have outlived their usefulness to television—more profitable spectacles like the World Series, the Super Bowl, and the Olympics could be used to promote technical and professional innovations. "ABC may be on the right track with their chintzy wrap-ups each night," said CBS President Robert Wussler, a former Convention producer himself. "Let's see how the Convention does tonight when ABC shows the All-Star Game. Politics or baseball—the ratings will be interesting."

The politicians had also looked over television's value to them. In March, the New York City Comptroller's office had come up with a proposal to sell the Convention to only one network—as the World Series and other sporting events were sold—or to charge each network $200,000 rent to bring their equipment into Madison Square Garden. Plans for an auction were discussed, and executives of CBS, NBC, and ABC were called into meetings—both CBS and ABC protested, saying that they would not pay for news, even though *Time* magazine and the *Des Moines Register* had to pay for their space in the Garden.

The plans were quickly killed by the Democratic National Committee and Mayor Beame's office. Cooler political heads were not about to tangle with network power. "What if they get mad? What if there were no bid? What if they pulled out? There might not be a Convention without television. People come to be seen. They come to get on television."

If the Convention was America, maybe the American Dream was getting on television. Joe Kaselak wasn't a nut; he was the primitive Jimmy Carter—or, at least, the pure Dick Celeste.

This was going to be Celeste's day in the American eye. He was at Madison Square Garden in the morning talking to himself on the podium. He was rehearsing the four-minute speech he was scheduled to make defending Paragraph E of Section III of the Rules Committee report.

"Debate without decision-making," he read to a hall empty except for cleaning men, police dogs, and such, "can too easily turn into posturing for the TV cameras. . . . A Constituency of Conscience demands more than debate. It demands a resolution of that debate by a vote—yea or nay. In our desire to be heard, and in our struggle to achieve change, let us not settle for less."

The words did not make a hell of a lot of sense, but that was the luck of the draw. Celeste, a member of Rules, had been assigned to rebut a minority report proposing that 20 minutes of debate be allowed on each of three issues if 300 delegates from 10 states filed a petition demanding discussion up to an hour before the Democratic platform was adopted by the Convention. There would be no vote taken after the 20-minute issue debates—the minority report itself was simply a device to get people on television without the consent of Robert Strauss. It was exactly the kind of noise-making move that Strauss wanted to keep out of the party rules, and Celeste was chosen to argue that, in the interest of openness, silence was golden. What he intended to do, of course, was to present himself to the nation for the first time in all his 6-foot-4 handsomeness, repeating over and over again his call for "A Constituency of Conscience"—whatever that meant.

Celeste was very nervous. Not about the speech, but about the timing. He was scheduled to mount the podium between 5:45 and 6:30 P.M. What that meant was that if he came on before six o'clock, CBS and NBC would still be covering Madison Square Garden and might pick up his call to conscience. But at six, the two networks would switch to their affiliate stations around the country for an hour of local news or game shows. On such schedules, he thought, rested the future of the Republic . . . well, of Dick Celeste, anyway.

Martin Jelin had made it. He logged more television time than any other New Jersey delegate, capping his celebrity with an appearance on NBC's "Today" show. A month before the Convention, the staff of "Today" had begun searching for a delegate who had been at the 1924 Democratic National Convention, the last one held in New York. They found Jelin, an asphalt manufacturer who had been a 14-year-old page at the two-week marathon meeting that nominated John W. Davis of West Virginia after 103 roll call ballots.*

Jelin, a wise man, had prepped himself for a round of television and newspaper interviews by reading whatever he could find on the 1924 meeting, and he displayed an encyclopedic memory of the events of 52 years ago: "The biggest difference between now and then is the beautiful colors and design of the place. . . . I remember very well the celluloid collar of Cordell Hull . . . Franklin D. Roosevelt getting up and calling Al Smith 'The Happy Warrior' . . . William Jennings Bryan being booed, then filling the Garden with his voice, thrusting away the microphone and saying, 'Take that instrument of the devil away from me.' " †

The booing of Bryan by crowds favoring the nomination of New York Governor Alfred E. Smith may have been the most significant event of that Convention; certainly it was not the nomination of Davis, who went on to a crush-

* The original Madison Square Garden—referred to by O. Henry as "the center of the universe"—was a converted old railroad shed on 26th Street near Broadway which opened as Barnum's Monster Classical and Geological Hippodrome in 1871 and became Madison Square Garden in 1874. The first building, dedicated to President James Madison, was demolished and replaced by a pseudo-Moorish garden designed by Stanford White—and it was there that White was murdered by Harry K. Thaw, the husband of showgirl Evelyn Nesbit. After the 1924 Convention, the Garden moved to Eighth Avenue between 49th and 50th Streets. The round Garden, built at a cost of $80 million, opened in 1968.

† Just as in 1976, there were sound problems at the 1924 Convention. One of the most enthusiastic demonstrations of the Convention began when Senator Pat Harrison of Mississippi said, "What this country needs is a Paul Revere." Anti-Prohibition delegates thought he had said, "What this country needs is real beer."

ing defeat by Calvin Coolidge. One of Jelin's sources— *The 103rd Ballot,* by Robert K. Murray—reported: "In the hinterland, Bryan's treatment by the New York galleries was considered little short of a national scandal. . . . The events of Wednesday afternoon must have shaken Bryan in his opposition to evolution, since every time he gazed into the galleries he must have become increasingly convinced of the existence of the missing link.

"Urban rowdyism was apparently New York's only answer to rural nativism and fundamentalism. . . . It was remarkable how little New York in 1924 really understood the rest of the country—how egotistical was the city's own view of itself and how badly it expressed its affection for Al Smith. As the taunts of the New York galleries again spread over the airwaves and crackled into the homes of Americans everywhere, it seemed to prove once more that New York's promises of hospitality and its claims of sophistication and tolerance were false indeed." *

That Convention, the first broadcast coast-to-coast, had helped set the mental picture of New York City for most of the country. Fifty-two years later, the people who ran and loved the town hoped to change that.

Stanley Friedman grabbed a cab in front of the Statler Hilton and said he wanted to go to the Americana. Unfolding his *Times,* he sneezed. The driver turned around and said: "God bless you."

At the Americana, the driver took his fare and said, "Have a good day, sir." What the hell was going on? Stan Friedman knew something about New York City—he was the deputy mayor—and he knew New York cabbies did not normally act that way; they wouldn't wish Queen Eliza-

* Robert K. Murray, *The 103rd Ballot* (New York: Harper & Row, 1960).

beth a good day. The town was really up for the Convention. Manhattan, the Bronx, and Staten Island, too, were trying to prove that they were part of America.

Friedman's city, the Big Apple, had some image. In response to queries from the city's Host Committee to delegation representatives, Alaska's had replied that their main concern was "just not getting hurt," and Indiana's had asked for "service for the men"—service? Yes, you know: women, prostitutes. Patrick Leahy, the executive director of the Ohio Democratic party, said that he would not need help—he was planning to assign male college students to escort women delegates on the streets if they left their hotel.

In fact, more than 6.5 million Americans lived in the five boroughs of America's greatest and most depressing city— many of them liked it and often got home at night without being mugged, raped, or run down by a taxi. Their problem was that, governmentally, they could not support themselves. The city was worn out. Its role as the greatest seaport and manufacturing center of the Northeast had been inevitably diminished by the economic decentralization of the country along new interstate highways and around airports and younger, more flexible cities with room to grow and build. Since World War II, the city had absorbed but not assimilated millions of unskilled blacks and Puerto Ricans driven north by the mechanization of agriculture and the city's extravagant promises of opportunity or liberal social benefits for the indigent. By the early 1970s, New York was no longer generating enough revenues to pay its bills —employee salaries and a dazzling range of welfare programs that seemed too generous by half to most Americans —and in 1975 only an emergency Federal loan program saved the city from municipal bankruptcy. There were a lot of hustles going on in New York during Convention Week, but the biggest one was by the shined-up city setting up

the Democrats, Jimmy Carter, and the rest of America for
the day when New York would come around to ask for
permanent subsidy—that would not be a bad deal in return
for the city's $5 million investment to get the Convention.*

Deal is both the name of a town on the Jersey shore and
what the state's politicians do for a living. Deal was the
town where Jersey City Mayor Frank Hague summered in
the 1930s and '40s. In the winter, when he was not in
Florida, he said things like, "*I* am the law." Hague's spiritual successor was State Senator James P. Dugan of Hudson County, who was the state Democratic chairman and
the strong man of the New Jersey delegation to the Convention. At the first delegation meeting someone accused
him of being a "boss" and he answered as Hague might
have: "Well, we need a strong hand at the tiller."

Jim Dugan and Jimmy Carter understood each other.
At their first meeting, in April, Dugan said he was for
Hubert Humphrey. "I appreciate your candor," Carter said.
"Tell me something: how is the New Jersey state chairman
picked and when is your term up?" Dugan then proceeded
to beat Carter's brains in. In the New Jersey primary on
June 8, Carter won only 25 delegates to 83 for a Dugan-led

* The city's costs, which were kept in check by daily monitoring by an
onsite auditing team headed by Deputy Comptroller Walter Prawzinsky,
broke down this way: $1.9 million for rental of Madison Square Garden;
$1.4 million for design and construction to turn it into a convention
hall; $280,000 to provide buses, cars, and parking for delegates and
DNC officials; $215,000 for insurance after the Garden refused to
accept self-insurance from the city's suspect general funds. Police overtime of $2.6 million was subsidized by a grant from the Federal Law
Enforcement Assistance Administration. The New York City Convention
Bureau estimated that the city investment was more than covered by an
estimated $8 million spent by Convention visitors—and hoped that favor-
able publicity would eventually generate future tourism and business
from more profitable conventions like the American Medical Association's.

slate that endorsed both Humphrey and Jerry Brown for president.

Carter came to the New Jersey caucus in the Jade Room of the Waldorf Astoria Hotel at 10:15 the second morning of the Convention. He enthusiastically grabbed Dugan and studiously ignored Governor Brendan Byrne, who had been the manager of that losing Carter campaign. The candidate made a 30-minute pitch for unity—"If we are divided, then we will suffer the self-imposed limitations from it"—and left.

After the meeting, Richard Samuel, a member of the Democratic National Committee and Dugan's chief lieutenant, gave a laughing account of what had happened to Nancy Bohning of the state Democratic Committee: "The press kept asking how many votes we'd cast for Carter. We told them 108. But, they kept saying, all these people kept saying they're for Brown. I said, 'They haven't been told yet.' "

Not only had they not been told, they had not been asked. Dugan, who now wanted to be Carter's man in Jersey, planned to cast all 108 of his state's votes for the nominee without polling his delegation.

In the Versailles Terrace of the Americana, Rosalynn Carter, the candidate's wife, was holding a press conference. Can Amy have a normal childhood in the White House? "I hope so. I think she has a normal childhood now."

That sort of thing usually attracts a few feature writers whose stories are wrapped around recipes. But sitting there taking notes were some of the most prominent political writers in the country—Anthony Lewis of the *New York Times,* Mike Royko of the *Chicago Daily News,* James Perry of the *National Observer,* and David Murray of the *Chicago Sun-Times.* "I feel guilty when I'm not doing anything," said Murray. "It seems to be the only thing going on. I am not a big fan of unity."

Section III of the proposed rules of the Convention read: ". . . The Call to future National Conventions shall promote equal division between delegate men and delegate women from each state or territory." There was a minority report filed to that section which substituted the word *require* for *promote*. The minority report language meant quotas, in this case a 50 percent quota. It also meant that the Women's Caucus—which met each morning at the Statler Hilton—had the power to ruin Bob Strauss's Convention and Jimmy Carter's week.

To avoid a messy, *televised* floor fight, Carter had been negotiating since Sunday with a self-appointed group of women leaders—Representative Bella Abzug of New York and National Committee member Patt Derian of Mississippi acted as their spokespersons—over the semantics of a compromise rule. On his way into services at the Fifth Avenue Presbyterian Church, Carter had told his personal assistant, Greg Schneiders, to call Chairman Strauss: "Find out what all these code words really mean. What is the history of 'all feasible steps'? What does 'the burden' mean? It sounds like 'the white man's burden.' " So, while Carter and his wife were singing "Blessed Assurance," Schneiders was on the phone in the minister's office trying to figure out what assurances the women wanted.

Not many, it turned out. Even though the number of women delegates had dropped since the 1972 Convention —from 38 percent to 34 percent—the Women's Caucus, or at least its leadership, was not anxious to bear the burden of disrupting unity week. The leadership, Strauss happily suspected, had its own agenda—Ms. Derian was a strong Carter supporter who wanted no trouble for her candidate, and Ms. Abzug was a Senate candidate and wanted a quiet, united party at least for a year.*

So, this morning in the Statler's Terrace Room, Bella Abzug and Patt Derian gave 1,000 women delegates and friends of the movement their assurances that "our demands have been responded to in full." Not met, but responded to—the word *promote* stayed in, but the promotion of equal division would take effect for the party's 1978 mid-term conference instead of the 1980 Convention. The fight was off, and Jane O'Reilly, sitting in the back of the room, wrote in her journal: "Bella, Patt, *et al.,* told us in the kindest possible, but nonetheless elitist, terms what they had decided we should accept. But we are gratified by our new status as insiders instead of petitioner outsiders."

Charles Kirbo, the slow-talking Atlanta attorney who was Jimmy Carter's most influential friend, was at the Sheraton talking again with John Glenn about the vice-presidency. At the same time, another Carter operative was interviewing Martin Sammon, a Cleveland lawyer who managed Glenn's 1974 Senate campaign, about charges that there had been anti-Semitic undertones that year in Glenn's primary campaign against Howard Metzenbaum, a Jew. Glenn, despite a feeling that his keynote disaster the night before might have ruined his chances, decided to spend the $229.49 that the New York Telephone Company charged for a special telephone and then give the number to one man, Jimmy Carter.

When the great Carter vice-presidential search had begun, it was a show for press and public. The candidate

---

* In 1972, operating under rules formulated by a Party Reform Commission headed by George McGovern, delegation selection procedures forcibly increased the number of women delegates from the 5 to 15 percent selected to attend conventions up until 1968.

had already made up his mind—at least, those closest to him were convinced he had and that he was going to choose Senator Frank Church of Idaho. But when Carter went through the motions of telephoning 30 "distinguished Americans" for their opinions of 24 names on his "possible" list, he kept hearing that Church was something of a wind-bag—the actual words were more polite. The men he kept getting good reports on were Walter Mondale and Glenn and, sometimes, Senator Edmund Muskie of Maine.*

The pseudosearch suddenly became quite real. Although Carter never told anyone exactly what he was thinking at any moment, long conversations in his living room in Plains in June and early July shifted focus over the weeks from Church to Glenn, then to Muskie and Mondale, and finally, in the days just before the Convention, to Mondale alone. It was a process of elimination and, like most political decisions, it was made negatively—day by day, Mondale seemed the least objectionable alternative. In those conversations, based on interviews with the contenders by Carter and Kirbo, telephone inquiries and an elaborate numerical rating by Hamilton Jordan and questionnaires filled out by the four senators, Carter memos rated the four finalists:

Church—"Good showing in the primaries . . . a light-weight."

Glenn—"Steady, popular, and hard-working . . . might

* The "panel of distinguished citizens" was a fancy name for the people who received telephone calls from Carter, Kirbo, and Hamilton Jordan to check out the 24 prospects. Among those called were: John Gardner of Common Cause; Ralph Nader; Derek Bok, the president of Harvard; Kingman Brewster, the president of Yale; columnist James Reston; Franklin D. Roosevelt, Jr.; and, ironically, Senator Muskie. Carter's staff also persuaded executives and reporters of Atlanta newspapers to check out the vice-presidential possibilities with journalists around the country, to see whether there were unpublished whispers of scandal in Minneapolis or wherever potential candidates came from.

appear too political because he appeared the least imaginative of the choices . . . could be problems because both J.C. and he were professional military officers . . . certainly not the most able of the group . . . problems with labor . . . personal finances, use of tax loopholes, etc.—the most complicated."

Muskie—"Able, respected, knows federal budget . . . Roman Catholic, might help . . . best of the 'old faces.' Wrong image?"

Mondale—"Most able, respected . . . would help with liberals and press. . . . J.C. is comfortable with . . . withdrew from presidential campaign, saying it was not worth it. Is he lazy?"

By Monday, the men closest to Carter were almost certain that he had settled on Mondale. But . . . he kept sending them out for more information on the others and even scheduled personal interviews in New York with three men who had been eliminated weeks before—Senators Henry Jackson and Adlai Stevenson III and Representative Peter Rodino. At least it kept the press busy.*

Kirbo also had some other business to take care of in New York. He had to see Edgar Bronfman, the president of Joseph E. Seagram & Sons, Inc.—Bronfman was one of a number of business giants who suddenly realized that their companies needed legal representation in Atlanta and that the best man to handle that work was the man closest to Jimmy Carter, Charlie Kirbo. And Kirbo wanted to see a Broadway musical, the musical of the season, *A Chorus Line*. Of course, tickets were impossible to get, but someone called the New York Host Committee and Mimi Gurbst of the committee called the Shubert Theatre for five tickets.

Within ten minutes, the public relations man for the

* The questionnaire filled out by Carter's vice-presidential prospects appears as Appendix B.

show's producer, Joseph Papp, called back. Five of the best orchestra seats were no problem at all. Mr. Papp would come to the theatre himself to make sure that Mr. Kirbo and his party were comfortable. By the way, Mr. Papp wondered if Mr. Carter would be in the Kirbo party.

By the time Ms. Gurbst got the five tickets, everyone at the Host Committee knew that Mr. Charles Kirbo, old friend of Mr. Jimmy Carter who might be the next president of the United States, was going to the theatre. Preston Robert Tisch, the chairman of the committee and president and chairman of Loews Corporation, said he would help Ms. Gurbst deliver the tickets—"Charlie Kirbo is a man I should know." Tisch, a man whose companies employ more than 200,000 people around the world, waited for 15 minutes on the guarded 20th floor of the Americana. But the only person he and Ms. Gurbst met was a messenger sent down from the 21st floor who traded $75 for the envelope containing the tickets.

Bob Strauss was on the phone with New York State Senator Manfred Ohrenstein, the leader of the Democrats in the state's upper house: "Listen, you little motherfucker. Stepping on my people is stepping on me, do you understand that? I care more about what comes out of that girl's ass than about your whole body, you cocksucker! Don't you dare come near the Convention. If I find out you're there, I'll have your ass in jail!"

Neil Walsh, New York City's deputy commissioner of public events, who had heard that through the open door of the chairman's office, said to Vera Murray, Strauss's executive assistant, "I guess this isn't a very good time to see him." Down the second-floor hall of the Statler Hilton, another listener stood pop-eyed. "I don't talk to people that way," said Chicago's Mayor Richard Daley.

Strauss had called Ohrenstein when he found one of his

secretaries, Sharon Nelson, in tears after a threatening harangue by the legislator who wanted, of course, extra credentials. The New Yorker had hit Miss Nelson just after Representative Thomas ("Tip") O'Neill of Massachusetts, the House majority leader, had finished screaming at her for more tickets: "You're deliberately humiliating me. When I think of all the things I've done for Bob Strauss and this is what I get in return!"

O'Neill went on the personal "Shit List" compiled by Kitty Halpin, the credentials chief and Strauss's former personal secretary, and her principal deputy, Rima Parkhurst. Also near the top of the list were the three "horribles"— Senators Harrison Williams of New Jersey, Claiborne Pell of Rhode Island, and Vance Hartke of Indiana, who daily and persistently threatened secretaries and volunteers who would not give them other people's credentials. Williams was rated the worst, probably because he had more pressure on him since it was so easy for his most important constituents to come across the Hudson River from Jersey for a night at the Convention. One of his ploys was to send staffers claiming to be relatives of Democratic National Committee employees. One said he was the cousin of Anthony Jackson, the supervisor of guest credentials, and was given a ticket by a young volunteer who then said, "Hey, Tony, your cousin is outside." Jackson came out and saw the Senate aide waiting at another credential window, trying to use his name again. The Williams courier was white. Jackson was black—and mad. He walked up to the Senate aide and snatched away the credential.

Kitty Halpin also had a personal list with one name on it—Fred Harris, a former Oklahoma senator and national committee chairman. Miss Halpin had been his secretary and he fired her. "He kicked me out because his wife thought we were sleeping together," she said. "I've never forgiven him." Tuesday afternoon, Harris asked for extra credentials—he had been given five a day as a one-time presidential candidate—and Miss Halpin sent out an assistant to say, "Miss Halpin says, 'No!' "

"Put on your pants, Tom—we've got company," Billy Carter said, knocking on the door of his buddy from Albany, Georgia, Tom Butler. The company was Myra Mac-Pherson of the *Washington Post,* interviewing the most easygoing of the Carters, the candidate's 39-year-old brother.

"I'm Billy, and I'm going to stay Billy. I'm not going to be the president's brother—he's driven enough for both of us. I'm going back home to Tom's house and hide in his pool and drink Pabst Blue Ribbon."

But Billy Carter, who liked to call himself a "redneck" and spent long hours of his days drinking beer with the boys at the gas station he owned in Plains, found that he liked the City of New York, walking miles through Manhattan at dawn: "I have never heard anything good about New York, and since I've been here I haven't seen anything bad."

At a party the night before in the Plaza Hotel, Billy had said to his sister, Ruth Carter Stapleton: "Let's just tell them the truth about Jimmy."

"What is the truth?" she said.

"I don't know."

Clare Smith had begun her Tuesday interviews at 10:30 in the morning, the first one in a bathrobe with a towel around her wet hair. The fifth one, just after noon, was "youngest delegates," with Charles Siegel of Washington, D.C. "Weird," Clare wrote. "We're both headed for the University of Chicago to study political science. But I'm two months younger than Siegel so I get all the attention. Too bad for him."

She just had time before the 1:00 P.M. bus to the Garden to run down Seventh Avenue to the Carnegie Delicatessen to stock up for an afternoon and night on the floor.

"Sit here, Clare," said Rick Weber when Clare kind of bounded onto the bus. He was a page for the Ohio delegation—"good-looking" was Clare's diary description—a 20-year-old Stanford University junior from Dayton. Clare told him about how hungry she had gotten the night before and gave him a corned beef sandwich. They laughed a lot and agreed to get together soon.

At 2:00 P.M., Charles Kirbo came to Strauss's office and the two of them walked around the corner to the McAlpin Hotel on West 33rd Street. It was not exactly their kind of place—the few guests there were fighting a losing battle against legions of mice and roaches—but it was Jerry Brown's style. Kirbo and Strauss were meeting with the governor of California—they wanted to see if the pimple was ready to pop.

The McAlpin was scheduled to close down forever on the day after the Convention and had already been deserted by two delegations that originally had chosen it—Oklahoma and Arizona—but Brown chose to hold court among the ruins rather than join the rest of the California delegation uptown at the New York Hilton.*

---

* Oklahoma's original selection of the McAlpin demonstrated the dangers of picking a place to sleep from 1,500 miles away. In the DNC's February draw for hotel preference, Oklahoma drew second choice and picked the McAlpin because it was so close to Madison Square Garden. Indiana had first choice, opting for the glamour of the Waldorf Astoria. The Waldorf was also a favored trysting place, being used by several political notables who booked rooms in two hotels. "James Gray," for instance, was actually a governor staying someplace else who wanted a room away from the eyes of the press—and of his wife.

"Nice place," Strauss said with a grin. That was about as far as the negotiations got between the chairman, Kirbo, the governor, and six young aides—"the acolytes," Strauss called them. Brown said that, after Wednesday night's roll call, he would be willing to make a motion that Jimmy Carter be nominated by acclamation. "We're going to recognize some well-scrubbed American to do that," Strauss said, thinking that this was the way Brown wanted to get to the podium and on television, maybe starting a movement for himself as vice-president. After the chairman left, Brown, who was usually pretty well scrubbed, asked his campaign manager, Mickey Kantor: "What did that mean?"

Perhaps Brown could have started something with one shot at television. Barbara Jordan had. The floor of room 2117 at the Americana was covered with 50 neat stacks of telegrams, and four women were opening Western Union envelopes, taking out more yellow messages and placing them on the stacks. They were all addressed to Jimmy Carter and said basically the same thing: Pick Barbara Jordan for vice-president.

There was pressure building, not enough yet, but a beginning. Jesse Jackson, the Chicago activist preacher, was on television saying: "If any white man or white woman did what Barbara Jordan did last night, the nomination would no longer even be a matter of discussion."

It was not a matter of discussion. Barbara Jordan had been on Carter's original list as a cosmetic gesture. He did not know—no one knew—how voters would react to a black or a woman, to say nothing of a black woman, on a national ticket, and he was not about to take the chance of finding out. In room 2127, Jody Powell, Carter's press secretary, was on the phone looking for Bob Strauss to get Representative Jordan to a press conference and stop this thing before it really got started. A professional by her own definition, she did what she was asked, telling the press that she hoped her supporters would respect her wishes and "endorse, as I will, the candidate chosen by Governor Carter."

In the office next to Powell, Alan Fein, the volunteer who had gone from the mailroom to guarding the portals of power, was taking a call from someone named Irving Lander, who identified himself as president of the World Frisbee Association. Mr. Lander said the association had seen a newspaper photograph of Carter throwing one of the plastic discs on his lawn in Plains and that, at this very moment, a case of 200 Frisbees was on its way to the Americana for the candidate.

John Kenneth Galbraith, professor emeritus of economics at Harvard, best-selling author, and former U.S. ambassador to India, was in town as a commentator for both the "Today" show and the British Broadcasting Corporation. But for the moment, his audience was smaller— he was regaling friends with imitations of eastern liberal types hinting of closeness to Jimmy Carter.

"I did run over his domestic program, but who knows . . ."

"Of course, on foreign policy, some of my ideas got into his thinking after . . ."

"I had lunch with him in Atlanta a couple of years ago and . . ."

Galbraith called his wife at their farm in Vermont and continued the routine, saying that everybody in town was afraid they might not recognize a Carter insider.

"Well, of course," she said, "you know Mrs. Carter, his mother."

"I do?"

"Yes, don't you remember? She came to see us in India when she was with the Peace Corps. She's a wonderful woman."

"Why didn't you remind me?"

Lucille Kelley, the New Hampshire chairwoman who knew the Carters, spent most of her afternoon at her favorite place in New York—Saint Patrick's Cathedral. She was a devout Catholic, and things had not gone well for her in recent months—her sister had begun chemotherapy treatments for leukemia, and she had spent more than a month in the hospital herself because of an automobile accident soon after the February 24 New Hampshire primary in which she had won her delegate seat. Carter had called her at the hospital and a nurse had come in to say: "A man keeps calling you, and when he was told that hospital policy does not allow phone calls in the rooms at night, he insisted that he was Jimmy Carter. Can you imagine?"

"I think," Miss Kelley said, "that it might be prudent of you and the hospital to put the next call through."

Mary Alice Elizabeth Ault was in Saint Patrick's at the same time as Miss Kelley—it was her favorite place, too. Ms. Ault, 22, once of Tucson, Arizona, once the wife of a dentist, usually stopped by the cathedral on her way to work at the Bottomless Pit. The business part of her day began in the middle of the afternoon with her daily make-up ritual in a studio apartment in Brooklyn Heights. An hour later she had been transformed—from a 5-foot, 8-inch, 115-pound girl Palmolive soap might have claimed as one of its own into a stark style she called "Early Tart." She popped two No-Doz, then headed for the Pit—the dancers who worked there, most of them lesbians, called it the "Snatch Pit"; the customers they called "the creeps."

"They think they're special, the assholes. You hate them

all," said a 22-year-old dancer who had come to New York and the Pit from Hawaii six months before. "At first I thought we were the lowest of the low, but they are—the creeps. At least we can think about the money."

"The place looks like a G-Y-N clinic," Mary Ault said. "Feet in the stirrups! Look at the girls, I hate them, humiliating themselves like that. They say they do it for the money, but they're going to pay it all out to shrinks in a few years."

The dancers looked down on the customers; Mary Ault looked down on the dancers. In a way their conversations were being repeated downtown at the Garden by politicians and reporters.

"The national news media have absolutely no interest in issues at all," said Jimmy Carter of the reporters who traveled with him. "What they're looking for is a 47-second argument between me and another candidate or something like that. There's nobody in the back of this plane who would ask an issue question unless he thought he could trick me into some crazy statement."

And James Wooten, one of the *New York Times*'s best political reporters, was in the press area telling a friend: "I sound like I admire the Carter people; actually I despise them. I know he doesn't believe that religious stuff. I know it! I know it! Southerners know he isn't a good ole boy or poor—he's the patrician of the town. His language is so subtle and smart. He thinks he's 99 percent smarter than anybody who's around him. He has no respect for scribes; he hates the press."

"There are ten thousand campaigns going on at this convention," said Greg Schneiders, Carter's personal aide, "and Jimmy Carter's is only one of them." Another one was Rick Neustadt's—he wanted to be a CBS correspondent.

Richard M. Neustadt, Jr., 29, the son of a well-known

Harvard political scientist, was one of the bright young men hustling around the periphery of American public affairs trying to decide, on a fairly high level, what he was going to do with himself. Like many young men and women who made up a kind of Junior League of the Establishment, he had dabbled in politics, the law, and journalism. A Harvard Law School graduate, he had practiced a while with one of Washington's more prestigious firms, and had taken leave to coordinate Morris Udall's campaign in Maryland before that fizzled. Now he was working his third pair of conventions for CBS. In 1968, Neustadt had been a "gopher"—go for coffee, go for paper clips—and four years later he was promoted to the intellectual life-support system designed to sustain Walter Cronkite's authoritative omniscience. He was back at this convention ten feet removed from the anchorman inside CBS's two-story, $400,000 anchor booth built over the Promenade Level seats at the end of the Garden.

Neustadt's basic job was to feed Cronkite index cards to keep him up to the minute on what was happening at the podium. Every two minutes during the Convention he would type a card out on a special typewriter with $\frac{3}{16}$-inch-high reading type. He placed each card—stating who was at the podium, what was being said and why—into a short chute to Mark Harrington, Cronkite's associate producer, who stood in a steel-lined pit hidden out of camera sight at the star's feet. Harrington would then scan the cards and hand them up to the anchor desk so that, at any moment, Cronkite could look down from his aerie and intelligently describe what was happening below.

Between cards, Neustadt watched Cronkite, waiting for queries—"Who's that?" . . . "What do we know about . . ."—then riffling through reference books and papers or his own memory before tapping out an answer or calling on the bank of writers and researchers in the long room behind the visible part of the anchor booth. To be ready—"alert" was a big word at CBS—Neustadt worked the Convention like any young reporter, looking for the stories and details that might set him apart. That was important, because like many upwardly mobile public affairs starlets, Neustadt did not want to leave the Washington–New York–Cambridge triangle. He hoped to win a network starring role without the usual apprenticeship as a correspondent in "the boonies," reporting fires and murders for a CBS affiliate in some place like Chicago. So, as the session began Tuesday afternoon at 1:30, he sent this result of his efforts down the chute:

FROM: *Neustadt*
TO: *Cronkite*
RE: *Confusion on Rules Fights*

Four floor fights are slated for this afternoon, and almost everyone is confused about them. The four issues are: standards for the 1978 mid-term conference; loophole primaries; lowering the 25% requirements for minority reports to 15%; and the role of the Judicial Council.

Few of the delegates understand these issues, and the debate this afternoon may not help much. At 12:30, an hour before the session is to start, the speeches were still being written. Most of the speeches for the majority side are being drafted by college interns. The Rules Committee office at the Statler Hilton is crowded with speakers asking questions about their speeches. I heard one speaker say, "I've read this thing, but I still don't understand what side I'm on."

The most confusing issue is the last: the role of the Judicial Council. The majority report—to expand the Council's authority—was scribbled on the back of an envelope at the Rules Committee meeting. Opponents now argue that the wording of the majority report, while expanding the power of the Judicial Council, may *eliminate* its authority over credentials challenges: its original function. Rep. Don Fraser, the man who wrote the majority report, admits that he worded it badly, but contends that no one intended to eliminate the credentials function, so it should not be read that way. Rules aficionados have noted that the majority report gives the Judicial Council the power to interpret party rules, so the Council could give itself back the credentials function.

Bewildered? So is everyone else. This is one reason the Carter forces are not taking a position on the Judicial Council—they don't understand it either.

What was confusing the Alabama delegation was a different set of rules—Jere Beasley, the state's ambitious young lieutenant governor, had broken them all by calling a press conference back home in Montgomery and accusing Governor Wallace of neglecting state government for years to chase the presidency. "The very people who talk about trimming the fat and too much government in Washington are the very ones who fight accountability here," Beasley said. "The best place to start restoring sanity to government is right here in Alabama."

So Jere Beasley, who used to make a point of being from the same little town as Wallace—Clio—and who was planning to run for governor in 1978, thought that ol' George was dead. He was not going to be the only anti-Wallace candidate in that field—former Governor Albert Brewer, Wallace's 1970 opponent, and Attorney General Bill Baxley, an old enemy, were both sure to run. What if there were a pro-Wallace candidate against that field? Some folks thought that would be the governor's wife, Cornelia. Larry Morris thought that would be Larry Morris.

"Hell, yes, I want to be governor," he said. "Everyone at the University of Alabama Law School wanted to be governor." But only tall, handsome, and articulate Larry Morris had been president of the school's student body in

1968, as he had been president as an undergraduate at Auburn, the state's other dominant university. Hell, he had told his high school civics teacher, who had shown the class a scrapbook of Alabama governors, that he should save a place for Larry Morris.

After graduating from law school, Morris apprenticed himself politically to a liberal, by Alabama standards, State Senator Thomas Radney. That ended when Radney was beaten badly in a 1970 race for lieutenant governor after the "Ubangi pamphlet" appeared—Radney was shown in a crudely pasted-up photograph standing among African tribesmen. The young lawyer then threw in with George Wallace, and now he wanted to join Massachusetts's Wallace delegates, whom he knew were circulating a petition to put the governor's name in nomination for president— under the new rules of the party, potential nominees had to approve a petition signed by 50 certified delegates from at least three states and the petition had to be presented to the secretary of the Democratic National Committee before 6:00 P.M. on the day before the nomination roll call. That was today.

The young state representative went to Madison Square Garden early, looking for Alexander Garnish, one of the petition carriers. By 3:30 P.M., the Wallace delegates had 70 signatures. Someone who knew Wallace had to talk to him, get him to sign the petitions before the 6:00 P.M. deadline. That someone was Larry Morris and he left the Garden with the petition at 3:45.

"If I were in charge," said Mazie Woodruff, the black grandmother in the middle of the North Carolina delegation, "I'd knock some heads together. Those people shouldn't be scuffling around in the aisles, making all that noise." She had worked months to get onto the floor of the Convention, and now she could barely hear what was happening. Senator Alan Cranston of California was giving the final report of the Credentials Committee at 4:25 P.M. to a half-empty, milling, buzzing hall.

"There was a collision this year between provisions in the rules imposing affirmative action obligations on state parties, and provisions in the rules giving candidates the right to approve their own delegates. The conflict caused bitterness in a number of states, and put several challenges before the Credentials Committee. We must resolve this conflict by 1980."

Hurley Goodall, in the Indiana alternate section, loved every word. He smiled and thought that he had been vindicated, that the long night ride from Muncie to Washington in his pickup to protest being bounced by the Carter deal with Indiana unions had been worth it—the same thing wouldn't happen to someone else in 1980.

But it might. Cranston, choosing his words carefully, had committed himself and the party to nothing. He defined Goodall's problem as a conflict between racial, sexual cosmetics and candidate strategy. The real problem, he was saying, was that a black man had been replaced by a white, not that citizens like Goodall in Indiana, North Carolina, and a dozen other states could, and did, work for months to build up a candidate's vote in primaries and precinct caucuses—and then find themselves arbitrarily eliminated from the process if the candidate decided to use those votes and the delegate seats they represented as patronage to deal with unions and party organizations or any other element of a state's power structure.

"Four years ago, thirty-two credentials challenges required public evidentiary hearings," Cranston said. "This year . . . only one public hearing was needed. In contrast to 1972, the committee has stayed out of the courts, and attracted very little publicity. And that's as it should be."

That was certainly the way Bob Strauss wanted it. "No matter how I did it, I was going to do the job I hired out to do," Strauss said. "The image was always on my mind: the Convention was going to be a montage of America—white faces, black faces, old faces, young faces, female faces. America was going to see us on television and see themselves. We were going to look and sound responsible—and get out of that hall by 12:30 each night."

At 4:30, inside the Garden with Mrs. Vanik's guest pass, Joe Kaselak went looking for Dan Troy, the young councilman he had gotten on NBC the night before. Friends at home had told Troy they had seen him, and the councilman was glad to scout the floor until he got Joe credentials of a delegate who planned to leave early.

Kaselak was on the floor for seven hours, making network cameras 12 times by his own count. He also made Cleveland television when a local reporter, Dave Patterson, noticed Kaselak's antics and decided to do a film report for showing at home the next night. And a Cleveland radio reporter, seeing Patterson interviewing Kaselak, came up and interviewed them both.

It was just after 4:30 when Larry Morris got into George Wallace's suite on the 39th floor of the New York Hilton. The governor, fully dressed, was sitting against the headboard of his bed, watching a taped interview with Senator Edmund Muskie on CBS.

"How you doing there, Larry?" Wallace said. "What can I do for you?"

Morris told him he could sign the petition and allow his name to go into nomination. "It's not for you, Governor. It's for your supporters. You heard them yesterday at the caucus. They deserve it."

Wallace was silent for a moment, then said: "I don't want anyone to accuse me of being the one who set off a brokered convention."

"You won't be. You're going to withdraw after the nominating speeches. This would just be for your supporters, the people who worked for you."

"Maybe you're right, Larry. Maybe we should do this. And then I would get up and tell my delegates to vote for Carter." Wallace took the petition and said, "Let me think on it for a little while."

Morris stepped out of the bedroom into a short hallway. He was now pretty sure that, within a few hours, he would be delivering a nominating speech on national television, establishing himself as the generational successor to George Corley Wallace.

A door opened down the hall and Cornelia Wallace came toward him. "Larry? What are you doing here?" she said. He explained. "Well, I completely agree with you," she said. "Completely." She went into the governor's bedroom and Morris heard her say: "George, I think it's completely appropriate. It's what you should be doing."

"Elvin," Wallace called to his assistant press secretary, Elvin Stanton. "Elvin, go get someone to get me up."

A black man was lifting Wallace to the side of his bed when Morris was called back into the room. "Larry, can you verify these names?" Wallace asked. Morris said that there was not time before the 6:00 P.M. deadline. "It would be a hell of a thing," Wallace said, "for me to sign this thing, have it sent over, and then have it invalidated.

"Larry, I'm skeptical," the governor continued. "If they turn around and invalidate it, it'll make us all look bad."

Morris argued that the agreement Wallace had with Chairman Strauss—that the chairman of the Alabama delegation, State Senator Robert Wilson, would be allowed to make a short speech from the floor praising Wallace before the state cast its presidential votes—was not going to do any good, that other delegates would begin to cheer or boo. The way for Wallace to be dignified, he said a little desperately, was to be nominated by his friends and then magnanimously withdraw.

"No," Wallace said. "No, Larry, I think we should forget it."

Just after 5 P.M., John Chancellor of NBC introduced a film of Jimmy Carter working on his acceptance speech, barefoot, biting on the end of his pen as he labored to put it to paper, yellow legal pads, in the dining room of his Americana suite. The film was the product of a 20-minute camera session in the morning—both still and television cameramen predictably opted for angles showing the candidate's naked toes.

Ironically, or inevitably in a media nation, at the same moment, the live Jimmy Carter was reading the speech for the first time to an audience—a select staff audience of Pat Anderson, Jody Powell, Greg Schneiders, Pat Caddell, and Jerry Rafshoon. It was very casual and Carter departed from the text occasionally, saying once after a phrase about changing leadership, "You can depend on it." He liked that and wrote it into the text.

There was a line that hailed "generations of immigrants" to the United States as "the best and the bravest" of the Old World. Someone argued that the words were historically inaccurate, that the immigrants were often neither the best nor the bravest of their countries. "Well," Carter said, "*you* go tell Pete Rodino his father was the worst"—but the line was killed.

The first draft of the speech had been written by Anderson during the last two weeks of June. The writer joined the campaign after the publication of a novel, *The President's Mistress*—the title told it all—but he had a deserved reputation as a talented political journalist and had served briefly as a low-level assistant in the Kennedy White House. Anderson was also respected by Carter, who had a simplistic view of reporters: if they said he was good, he thought they were good. Reading a favorable column, he would say, "I think Reston is beginning to understand what's happening." And Anderson had written a rhapsodic piece about Carter in the *New York Times Magazine* in December, 1975—when it counted.

Anderson, who lived near Washington, traveled to Carter's home in Plains on July 1 with a first draft. The candidate read it that day and suggested that Anderson make some calls around the country—"get bright people, young people." Carter wrote his own version over the Fourth of July weekend, plugging in ideas that Anderson was picking up in his telephoning, which tended toward old Kennedy writers like Theodore Sorensen and Adam Walinsky. Carter's draft—25 handwritten pages on legal pads— was finished on July 9, three days before the Convention. Anderson reworked that, smoothing out the language, and on the day before the Convention gave the candidate the third draft—the one Carter was editing on-camera.

Anderson showed that draft to Milton Gwirtzman, a Washington attorney and onetime Kennedy writer who quadrenially managed to get aboard the campaign plane of almost every Democratic candidate for president so that he was usually somewhere around the winner. Gwirtzman consulted with Sorensen and Walinsky—each of whom had gotten a couple of sentences into the speech—and then pronounced his judgment: "This is terrible. Carter can't give this speech. It's just not presidential."

"But," Anderson said, "this is Jimmy's. He wrote most of it."

"There are some things," said Gwirtzman, who had written for Robert Kennedy, Hubert Humphrey, and George

McGovern, "that are too important to be left to the candidate."

"Hey, Mom, guess where I am?" Richard Bonsignori, a 28-year-old lawyer from Somerville, New Jersey, said from a public phone in the lobby of Madison Square Garden. "Yeah, watch for us on television." Bonsignori and his wife, Theresa, had walked around the Garden, just to see what was going on, and a woman had handed them "Guest" credentials.

The Democrats were padding the house. Television had shown about 3,000 empty seats in the stands on Monday night, even though more tickets were distributed than there were seats. Nobody seemed to be able to figure out how to mesh credential supply and demand. While state delegation chairmen were pleading for more tickets on the second floor of the Statler Hilton, the things were being handed out to anyone who walked by on the other side of Seventh Avenue. The Convention's security triumvirate— Cliff Cassidy, Jim McDonnell, and Miami Beach Police Chief Rocky Pomerance, a consultant—had absorbed Chairman Strauss's anger about the untelegenic empty seats and at 2:30 that afternoon decided to shoot the works. Their plan was to issue every available "Guest" pass—40 percent more than they had seats for—plus 1,500 extra pink "Operations" credentials, normally used by messengers and Madison Square Garden employees. Convention aides were then ordered to guide "Guest" pass holders to the least desirable "Honored Guest" seats on Level 7 of the Garden and put the "Operations" holders into Mezzanine "Guest" seats on Level 9—Level 8 had no public seating, just 22 "Skyboxes," plush glass-fronted rooms that rented to corporations for $55,000 a year, but were reserved now for security operations, radio stations, and very special guests, usually Bob Strauss's.

Pomerance, who was sort of responsible for Bonsignori's phone call home, happened to be across the lobby, talking with friends. "Rocky!" cried a pretty young woman, hurrying toward the 300-pound police chief. "Rocky? You don't recognize me? I'm Shari Whitehead."

"Shari! How are you? It's been four years," he said, telling the people with him that they had met when she was a leader of demonstrators at the Miami Beach Convention, demonstrators who felt George McGovern was just another Establishment politician. "What are you doing here?"

"I'm a delegate. From California."

"You see?" said Pomerance, an enthusiastic man who not only seemed to have no enemies, but whose adversaries always seemed friendly. "I told you, then, when you were fasting to protest bombing of North Vietnam. Now, tell me, does it work? Does the system work?"

"No. This is a dull sham of democracy. I'm here trying to create a critical voice—to wake these people up," she said, hurrying off cheerfully. "We're just *using* Jerry Brown and Cesar Chavez to try to get our message across."

It was loser's night on the podium. First George Mc Govern, the party's candidate in 1972, then Hubert Humphrey, the candidate in 1968, then George Wallace. McGovern, the senator from South Dakota who had suffered the worst general election defeat in American history, came on at 7:38—22 minutes before prime television time would begin on the East Coast. That was something like the story of his life. His 1972 acceptance speech in Miami Beach had begun at 3:00 A.M. Eastern Daylight Time— midnight on the West Coast—because that chaotic Convention had debated issues like gay rights and abortion far into the night.

He was applauded for a minute and, in the California delegation, Susan Welsh of Los Angeles interpreted the reception as "Yes, George, we remember and we appreciate. No, George, we're not going to listen."

They always listened to Humphrey—for a while, anyway, because he could talk longer than most people could listen. It had been another sad year for the Happy Warrior, the man who had won the party's nomination while America watched Chicago police clubbing antiwar demonstrators outside the Convention hall—and a bare majority of Americans then elected Richard Nixon as their president. Humphrey had run again in 1972, savagely attacking his old friend, McGovern, in the primaries, and in 1976 had waited for, and done his best to promote, a brokered Convention that might turn to him as the nominee—even though he knew he was facing cancer surgery. Instead, he ended up playing elder statesman at a Convention dedicated to a man who was getting elected to the Sumpter County, Georgia, school board when Humphrey ran for president for the first time in 1960.

On the floor, Fritz Efaw, the draft evader from the Democrats Abroad delegation, was in the New York delegation looking for Ramsey Clark, who had been attorney general of the United States when Efaw was first indicted in the last days of Lyndon Johnson's presidency. Clark was a candidate for the U.S. Senate in New York but, more importantly, he had become a prominent symbol of respectable left-wing politics. Clark almost never said no. If Hubert Humphrey had more solutions than there were problems, Ramsey Clark spoke for more causes than there were committees.

"Would you nominate me for vice-president?" Efaw asked Clark.

"Yes. I would be proud to."

The idea of nominating Efaw for vice-president to get television time to promote amnesty for Vietnam War resisters had been worked out at a party the night before the

Convention in the apartment of Sarah Kovner, a director of the National Council for Universal and Unconditional Amnesty. There was a sadness and frustration at that affair. Mrs. Kovner and many of her guests had been national powers behind the presidential candidacies of Eugene McCarthy and George McGovern; then, they had thought they were taking over the Democratic party. But in 1976, their many candidates, Mo Udall the last of them, had divided their strength and been conquered by Jimmy Carter. The national spokesmen of 1968 and 1972 had been reduced to collecting 50 delegate signatures from at least three states to win some network time for a man who was six years too young to hold national office. And, because Efaw was younger than 35, the constitutional minimum for presidents and vice-presidents, Robert Strauss planned to rule the nomination out of order to keep "that weirdo" off the podium.

In the unkindest cut of all, while Humphrey spoke, ABC, televising baseball's All-Star Game from Philadelphia, was showing President Gerald Ford in the stands singing "The Star Spangled Banner"—and more than 50 million Americans were watching that. Inside Madison Square Garden, maybe 15,000 Democrats and guests applauded Humphrey for four enthusiastic minutes. In the North Carolina delegation, C. J. Hyatt, a real estate broker who had been George Wallace's state campaign manager, was outraged. He saw reporters clapping in the aisles and shouted: "Hey, I thought you were newsmen. If you think he's such a great speaker, you write about it. But you've got no business clapping and carrying on here."

The Bottomless Pit was doing two waves of Convention business—late afternoon–early evening and postsession— and it was selling more Jack Daniel's than it ever had before. "They're all crackers," said Mary Ault, waving disgustedly at a wall of men wearing "Carter" buttons. "This place is for high-class perverts."

Chez Paree, directly across Seventh Avenue from the Americana Hotel, had the same late afternoon and post-session pattern of business, with one difference: Convention people would walk in between 5:00 and 7:00 P.M. and quickly turn around, repelled; but many of them would be back late at night, often drunk. There were dancers on the bar—heavier and older women than at the Pit—and men's hands reached for them. There was "no touch" at the Bottomless Pit because liquor was served, and the State Liquor Authority could challenge the club's license for lewdness. Chez Paree had already lost its liquor license and was serving a two-ounce glass of Coca-Cola at $3.75 a glass. There was "touch" at Chez Paree—dancers and customers were head down on each other's crotches along the walls.

A dancer named Suzie, wearing her dyed red hair in pigtails, dropped her heavy breasts in front of a young man in a suit wearing "Delegate" credentials and the inevitable "Carter" button. "Touch my tits," she said, then she moved his hand slowly down between her legs. "Good boy. Stick your finger up there. . . . It's just a little tight. I haven't had it for eight months. Ohhh!

"Now give me a dollar," she said. The man didn't move. "I need a dollar.

"Look, kid," she said, her voice changing, "you want to touch, you gotta pay."

Suzie moved along the bar to another man, turning and shoving her backside into his face. "Stick your tongue in my ass." He hesitated for a second, then did it. The men at the bar stood and cheered, and he gave her a dollar. The young man with the "Delegate" tag came down the bar, this time waving a dollar.

"Too late, kid," Suzie said, but he persisted, reaching toward her with the money.

"Fuck off!"

Lynda Bird Johnson Robb took a seat in the VVIP section and soon noticed Paul Newman sitting across the aisle. He took about four and a half seats, with his legs and arms spread around him. Mrs. Robb asked one of Mark Gasarch's ushers to ask Newman to come over, she would like to meet him. Gasarch told the usher to try— "I guess she thinks her father is still president"—and see what happened.

What happened was that Newman looked up at Mrs. Robb, smiled, and then turned to the usher and said, "Fuck her."

At 8:45 P.M., Mary McGrory, the Pulitzer Prize–winning political columnist of the *Washington Star,* said excitedly: "Mark Fidrych is on next!"

Mark Fidrych, nicknamed "Bird," was a 21-year-old pitcher for the Detroit Tigers who had won eight games and lost one, which was good, and was something of a flake who talked to the ball, which was better. He was the biggest attraction of the All-Star Game. Miss McGrory was in the middle of 100 reporters crowded around one of the three televisions—the one tuned to ABC—in the Railroad Lounge, a curtained-off area outside the arena where the Association of American Railroads thought it good business to provide free food and drink for reporters at a daily rate of 400 cups of coffee, 500 glasses of soda, 1,600 glasses of beer, and 7,000 little ham, turkey, roast beef, and corned beef sandwiches.

If you are what you eat, the pecking order in Madison Square Garden was: delegates on the bottom, then print and local electronic reporters in the middle, and network people, diplomats, assorted celebrities, and friends of Bob Strauss on top. All the delegates had access to were 13 concession stands run by H. M. Stevens, Inc., which feeds 35 million sports fans around the country each year—being a representative of the folks back home meant that delegates had to pay 50 cents for the same finger sandwiches being given out free to reporters, and that they could not buy beer, which the DNC had banned from sale for the week.

The television networks catered hot meals for their employees—better than sandwiches even if, for some reason, NBC's string beans were rejected by metal-detecting security devices one night. The best of everything was reserved for the Diplomats' Lounge—80 of the 150 ambassadors to the United States attended the Convention—and three areas controlled by Strauss: the Skyboxes at the top of the Garden; the chairman's "Help" lounge behind the podium; and the VIP Lounge in the building's Sports Hall of Fame, usually reserved for Knick and Ranger season-ticket holders. Stevens catered to the diplomats and Strauss guests, too—but the 85-cent hot dogs were replaced by steak tartare, crab quiche, smoked turkey, and Chivas Regal.

The "Help" room was a cocktail lounge, usually reserved for reporters covering the Knicks and Rangers who found it inconvenient to leave their drinks, television, and Garden publicity handouts during basketball and hockey games. "Now I know why sportswriters aren't as mean as political writers," Strauss said when he first saw the room. "I'll use this for people who help me, like reporters from Dallas who write stories about what a great job Strauss is doing. Then we'll sprinkle a few senators and governors in here to impress people who help the party."

Admission to both the Skyboxes and the VIP Lounge was controlled by Strauss and DNC Finance Chairman S. Lee Kling. Unfortunately for Strauss and Kling, a St.

Louis banker, the VIP Lounge became one of the Convention's great challenges. Reporters sneaked in regularly through the kitchen to mingle with the likes of Mrs. Walter Cronkite and Iranian Ambassador Ardeshir Zahedi, and 100 of the lounge tickets were stolen the first night of the Convention. While Mark Fidrych was pitching—the lounge had 12 television sets—Speaker of the House Carl Albert complained that reporters and photographers were getting in, trying to get pictures of him with a glass in his hand and write more stories about him drinking too much. All he had in his glass, he said, gesturing to a woman seated next to him, was lemon and water. Lee Kling came up to the Speaker with a photographer and asked if the Speaker would pose for a picture with Mrs. Kling.

Albert got up and stood next to the finance chairman's wife, but the photographer didn't move, and the Speaker asked why. "Mr. Speaker," he said, "I was hoping you'd put your glass down for this shot."

Bob Strauss promised George Wallace a prime-time television appearance—and he got it. Sort of. The crippled governor waited in his wheelchair at the back of the podium as Strauss came forward to introduce him at 9:21 P.M.—a time deliberately selected so that America would have to choose between a fading politician and All-Star baseball—but first the chairman dramatically pointed out Jacqueline Kennedy Onassis in the VVIP boxes.

There were cheers across 33rd Street in the NBC control room, connected to the Garden by clusters of 900-foot-long cables. CBS was "out"—their coverage was interrupted for a commercial—so NBC had Jackie and CBS had a Ford Mustang. "Zoom in on her face," yelled Robert Mulholland, the executive vice-president of NBC News, one of seven men facing 14 flickering television monitors.

Their "room" was actually a 60-foot trailer attached to seven smaller trailers parked on the plaza area of an office building across the street from the Garden—a plaza rented for $45,000 for the Convention.

Wallace was wheeled on at 9:24. At that moment, the Convention was being watched by less than 20 percent of the national television audience. Most Americans were watching ABC—the All-Star Game was in the fourth inning and Tom Seaver of the New York Mets was pitching to Fred Lynn of the Boston Red Sox, a classic confrontation between a great veteran and a spectacular young hitter.

In Philadelphia, Lynn hit a Seaver curve ball into the right field stands for a home run. In New York, standing at the standard of the New York delegation, Bill vanden Heuvel was urging impassive liberal delegates: "C'mon, applaud. Give Wallace a hand." The Alabaman had been speaking for two minutes when Gordon Manning, the executive producer in the NBC control trailer, said, "I think that's about enough of Jackie"—and the network cut to the same Ford Motor Company commercial that CBS had shown five minutes before, coming to Wallace at 9:28.

Hurley Goodall, the determined Indiana alternate, applauded Wallace from the moment he appeared. The two men had never met, but Goodall had once risked his job over George Wallace. In 1968, Wallace had come to Muncie to speak in a state university building and local blacks planned a demonstration to protest his use of a public building because he had denied the right of blacks to use segregated public facilities in Alabama. At that time, the city had a law prohibiting its employees—including firemen —from participating in demonstrations of any kind. Goodall had gone to the fire chief and said—"I didn't ask"—that he was going to picket Wallace. "When I became a fireman," he said, "I didn't give up my citizenship. I've got two kids who look me in the face every morning." Nothing was ever said again about the incident.

Eight years later, in Madison Square Garden, Goodall was saying, "I watched Martin Luther King's father shake Wallace's hand before he spoke. Something significant happened at that moment. Maybe we'll all come out all right. We've passed through a lot of bitterness—now maybe we can deal with each other person-to-person."

In the Alabama section, delegation chairman Bob Wilson was on the red phone to the podium, complaining that no one could hear their governor—"What is wrong with the sound?"

One thing that was wrong was that Wallace, in a wheelchair, could not get close enough to the microphones. He had wanted to wear a lavaliere—a small microphone worn like a locket—but the Garden's chief electrician, Norm Leonard, vetoed that because the sound of his voice would have fed directly into the Pool audio system and then into the Garden's public-address system, bypassing the IBEW-installed podium microphone and the IBEW-operated amplifiers. That was what the jurisdictional dispute that had brought detectives into the Garden was about.

While Wallace spoke, Leonard and Mickey McCauley of the Garden were arguing again with Steve Alper of the Pool, who accused Leonard of deliberately distorting the sound, saying that he had seen the chief electrician signaling his men to cut back volume and power when the sound in the Garden got too good.

"There was no sabotage during the session," McCauley said. "My men were angry and there was some during rehearsals, but they would be fired if I caught them doing it now, and I've got men all over this building looking over their shoulders. No one would take the chance—our electricians average $35,000 a year in a business that has 66 percent unemployment. Use your head."

Jacqueline Kennedy Onassis, attending her first Convention since John Kennedy's nomination in 1960, spread awe in her path and chaos in her wake. When she arrived, photographers charged the Missouri delegation like a strobe light brigade—the Missourians just happened to be seated directly in front of Loge 57, the VVIP section. Mrs. Annetta St. Clair, a 38-year-old political science instructor at Missouri Southern State University, was knocked from her chair by an infantryman of United Press International. Standing on her chair, he clicked away at Mrs. Onassis; standing on the floor, Mrs. St. Clair clicked off self-portraits with the 35mm Nikon at his hip.

"What the hell are you doing?" he screamed when he felt his spare camera bouncing around. "I'm working, lady."

"Oh, you are?" she said. "Well, I am, too. I was elected by the people of Newton County, Missouri, to represent them here. Now, get off my chair!"

The most famous woman in the world took Mark Gasarch's arm. She had decided she wanted to talk to Mayor Richard Daley and, using walkie-talkie unit 20, which he had come to think of as a phallic symbol, the young lawyer had cleared her way to Bob Strauss's hideaway office under the podium. With the eight security people assigned to his guest, Gasarch walked her to an elevator being held to take her from the sixth to the fifth level of the Garden. The security men, Mrs. Onassis's sister, Lee Radziwill, and her escort, Peter Tufo, and Gasarch rushed into the elevator as the doors began to close—leaving Mrs. Onassis outside. Gasarch jammed his arm into the doors to force them back open.

Mrs. Onassis and Daley, the florid old pol who had helped

make her husband and Jimmy Carter the leaders of the party, talked privately for ten minutes—alone, except for Gasarch, the Strauss family, and 14 security men. When it was obvious that their conversation was over, it was also obvious that if Mrs. Onassis and her security detail walked into the little hallway outside and ran into George Wallace's entourage leaving the podium, there was going to be a collision between two irresistible forces. Rick Strauss, the chairman's son, tried to solve that by taking pictures of Mrs. Onassis and Daley until it seemed safe to leave; he kept shooting even after his film ran out. They left and turned left—into a phalanx of Alabama state troopers clearing the way for their wheeled leader. Their technique was simple: anybody who got in their way was smashed into the wall. Thwock! Thwock! Thwock!—people were flattened. Mrs. Onassis cringed against the wall waiting for her turn—and it came as a large arm swung toward her, then froze. So did the face behind the arm: *Jackie Kennedy!* The trooper moved on, giving the next body, Gasarch, a double-Thwock!

When Jackie decided to leave, the security people decided that the best way to handle it was to take her on an elevator to the second level and then activate a guarded escalator to a ground-level entrance where her car waited. A Garden employee was called with the key to the escalator —which was shut down for security reasons—and he was so nervous he couldn't get the key in the switch. "Now! Now, John!" . . . "Here she comes" . . . "Hurry, Hurry!" She was 20 feet away when John got it moving—up. "It's going the wrong way, John!" She was paying no attention, chatting with her friends, and stepped on the escalator— at that instant John got it going down. Mark Gasarch, touching his cheek where Jackie had kissed him to say thank you, wondered whether she thought that escalators automatically went down if she stepped on them.

At 9:45, the "line" screen in the NBC control trailer—the screen showing what network viewers were actually seeing—showed Bess Myerson, New York City's former consumer affairs commissioner, reading sections of the Democratic platform. The other 13 screens in front of the seven NBC executives showed five shots inside the hall, six shots outside, mainly at the hotels of vice-presidential prospects, and the line feeds of the competition, CBS and ABC. There were 48 more screens in smaller trailers to the left and right of the control group—the best of those shots by NBC—and Pool cameras were the ones moved on to the central screens. "What have we got inside?" said Lester Crystal, the convention producer and the man who actually decided what went on line. "Lowenstein or the funny man," said the inside producer, Joseph Angotti.

"We need some comic relief after this," said Gordon Manning, the executive producer. "Cut this. Give me the funny man," said Crystal into the small microphone on the control panel in front of him. The funny man was a Georgia delegate named Sam Way, who was wearing a Jimmy Carter mask and had been standing next to correspondent Tom Pettit for 20 minutes waiting for this chance. Way ripped off the mask and started to give a serious analysis of the state of the Democratic party and the nation. Pettit broke in and said: "Okay, Sam, put it back on."

At 10:00 P.M., the NBC line was showing Jerry Wurf, the president of the American Federation of State, County, and Municipal Employees, reading another section of the platform, and Angotti said that correspondent Tom Brokaw had been holding Senator Frank Church for three minutes.*

---

* The platform was read by a series of 20 speakers ranging from Mayor Richard Daley of Chicago to Coretta King, Martin Luther King's widow. Originally, Robert Strauss had accepted the advice of the Demo-

10:05 P.M.—Wurf finished speaking and Ray Lockhart, the NBC producer setting up options for Crystal's cuts, applauded slowly, saying, "Thank you. Thank you." David Brinkley came on the live monitor using some information collected during the day by his spotter, Mark Shields—that the public employee unions had helped elect 181 of their members, mainly schoolteachers, as convention delegates. Crystal leaned over to Manning and said, "Jesus, that's scary." Brokaw was still holding Church, who was scowling and pushing away red-and-blue streamers that kept blowing into his face from the Idaho State standard.

10:09—"Give me Church," Crystal said, and almost miraculously, the sulking image on the inside monitor switched to a grinning, animated Senator Church on the line screen.

10:21—Steven Flynn, NBC's vice-president of sales, sitting behind Manning, said, "You have to get three commercial breaks in before eleven o'clock."

The most exclusive stairway in New York was the fire exit between the 20th and 21st floors of the Americana, decorated with some tan paint, a coiled hose, and cigarette butts. It was the path from a guarded desk in the hallway of the 20th floor to the inner sanctum of Jimmy Carter, his very large family, and closest staff.

Kathleen Blithe and Jacquie Hyland, two high school freshmen from California visiting New York on a school tour, appeared at the 21st-floor doorway at 10:45 P.M., running into Carter's personal assistant, Greg Schneiders. They wanted to know if they could get a couple of Carter

---

cratic National Committee's television consultant, former CBS producer Al Vecchione, that 6 was the maximum that the networks would give sustained coverage. But week by week, apologizing to Vecchione each time, Strauss added names to repay old political debts and create some new ones.

buttons and maybe say hello to Jimmy. "How did you get here?" Schneiders asked with a laugh. "We took the elevator to the 22nd floor," Kathleen said, "then we walked down."

Ken Forsch of the Houston Astros took care of the American League All-Stars one, two, three in the ninth inning and at 10:50 P.M. the National League had the game won, 7 to 1. Half of the Americans with televisions turned on were watching the game, according to ratings released later, while only 15 percent watched Convention coverage on CBS and NBC—the rest watched old movies or whatever else local stations were showing between 8:00 and 11:00 P.M., prime time.

Almost no one, even in Madison Square Garden, was watching or listening to Mary King as she read the health care sections of the Democratic platform. Ms. King, a Washington health consultant who emphasized her old ties to Jimmy Carter, was chosen after Senator Edward Kennedy declined the honor of being one among the 20 Democrats reciting bits of the platform. The offer had to be a calculated insult or an indication that Carter had no intention of sharing any of the glory of his ascension with the most glamorous figure in the party, the heir to the legacy of Jack and Bobby—if there was going to be any legacy post-Carter. On the day Carter announced his candidacy for president, December 12, 1974—at the time, it hardly seemed a date worth remembering—he stopped by Kennedy's office to ask the 42-year-old senator's plans. Kennedy told Carter the same thing he had been telling the newspapers, that under no circumstances would he run. That's good, Carter replied, because there will be time for you after I've served eight years in the White House. Kennedy must have had a good laugh with friends after the incredibly confident Georgian, whom he had met only once before, left the office to go on to press conferences where nobody would show up.

But Kennedy was not laughing in New York. He had spent part of his evening at a party in an apartment overlooking the East River, making light conversation: "I'm having trouble getting a perimeter pass to the Convention." The party was hosted by one of New York's most elegant and powerful women, Mary Lasker, and the guest of honor was House Majority Leader Tip O'Neill, who was tall, heavy, and red-faced, the very model of an old Boston Irish politician.

"I can see why the Carter people didn't want Teddy walking around their Convention," said Jane O'Reilly. "All he had to do was walk in the room, and I felt incandescent —and I don't even like Teddy."

"It's sad, I guess," said a congressman. "If Carter wins, in four years, Kennedy will be Tip O'Neill."

10:58—Mayor Richard Daley of Chicago finished reading his section of the platform and NBC went to a Textron commercial, the last one scheduled for the hour. "It's under the wire," Gordon Manning said in the control room. "You cut it very close," said Steve Flynn, the sales vice-president.

11:25—Correspondent Cassie Mackin came on the NBC line with actor Paul Newman, saying that he had great interest in energy policy and breaking up oil companies. No one in the control room could understand what he was trying to say. Bob Mulholland finally said, "He's drunk!" Crystal went to a Colgate toothpaste commercial.

The Pool monitors showed that the only demonstrators outside the Garden were a couple of dozen Yippies, camped disconsolately on the steps of the New York Post Office on Eighth Avenue. Dan Courtenay, the city's top cop on the scene, was recommending that his force of 1,500 men be reduced to 1,200 for the rest of the Convention. So far, his officers had made exactly two arrests—Bennett Masel and Miriam Schlinger, two Yippies, who had been picked up for using a loudspeaker without a permit when they refused to stop heckling antiabortion marchers on Sunday.

A New York radio reporter began to interview Lucille Kelley, the New Hampshire chairwoman, just after 11:30. But they couldn't hear each other very well as delegates began to applaud and cheer for Senator Frank Church at the podium. "Let's crouch down," he said, and they did, but he lost his balance and toppled toward the chair holding up the Iowa standard.

Miss Kelley heard a scream. The next thing she heard was a voice, her own, saying: "My head. My head. Part of my head is gone . . . Please. Please, don't take pictures. Don't take pictures. My sister will see . . ."

The 13-foot high, 70-pound Iowa standard had fallen, the sharp edges splitting open Lucille Kelley's head. She could not see, but there was noise, shouting and screaming all around.

"I'm a doctor. Let me through there. Let me through."

"Stop him! That man has no credentials. He shouldn't even be here."

"But I'm a doctor. That woman is . . ."

The next thing Miss Kelley heard was a siren. She was in an ambulance. "Don't tell the Carters," she said. "Don't let the Carters know about this."

She passed out again.

Most of the Ohio delegation went back to the Sheraton before 11:00 P.M. Paula Slimak from Cleveland's Channel 5 came into the hotel bar and said she wanted to do a "Convention isn't all work" piece. Cleveland Councilman Benny Bonanno and Beth Farnsworth agreed to dance for the camera, then Councilman Earle Turner asked Clare Smith to dance. The television floodlights went on and Clare imagined a conversation with her mother after the film showed back home.

"Clare, what were you doing in a bar in New York?"

"Dancing, mother."

"Why were you dancing?"

"Music was playing."

"Why were you dancing with a councilman?"

"He asked me to dance."

"Why was he black?"

"Probably because his parents were, Mom."

11:50—The line monitor in the NBC trailer showed correspondent Edwin Newman interviewing Daniel Patrick Moynihan, former U.S. ambassador to the United Nations and a Senate candidate in New York. Because Newman was not wearing a headset or earpiece, a sign was held up off-camera to signal him to cut off the interview. The monitor showed Newman scratching his nose, an NBC on-air signal that he had seen the sign. "He's got it," Manning said.

11:57—Joe Angotti, the inside producer, called to Crystal: "I've got Cassie standing by with Pat Caddell. He's going to say that it's all bullshit, that the vice-presidential thing isn't down to just Mondale and Muskie."

12:02 A.M.—"We've got three gum chewers," said Angotti. "Let's see 'em," said Manning, and the line monitor switched back and forth between three cameras focused on jaw-working delegates.

12:19—"There's an extra commercial that sales would like to run," Lockhart told Crystal. "Okay," he answered, "but let's concentrate on what we're going to do. The gavel comes down, and then we'll do the wrap-up."

12:22—NBC went out for the commercial. The closing gavel banged at 12:25, and the network missed it.

12:27—Chancellor called on his floor correspondents for their "summaries" of the night's work. "My summary," said John Hart, "is submission. And I submit to you, Cassie."

A little after midnight, Tom Hayden and his wife, Jane Fonda, were on the sixth floor of 30 Rockefeller Center waiting to appear on NBC's "Tomorrow" show—the former radical leader, a California alternate pledged to Jerry Brown, was good media partly because he was one of the people at the Convention still willing to publicly criticize Jimmy Carter. The guest before them turned out to be the candidate's 77-year-old mother, Lillian Carter. "Miss Lillian" hurried out of the elevator, rushed up to Ms. Fonda, and hugged her, saying, "I'm proud to meet you. I wouldn't trade this moment for anything."

"And that fine young man," she said, looking at Mr. Hayden, "if he decides to run for office again and there's anything I can do to help, please ask me—if you want me to come out . . ."

Tom Snyder, the show's host, was surprised later that neither Mr. Hayden nor Ms. Fonda had a single unkind word to say about Miss Lillian's son. "The southern liberal," Hayden said, "has a certain kind of integrity that's almost impossible to achieve in the North."

Miss Lillian, as usual, was delightful: "Sometimes I have five interviews in one day. That's too many. But when people come and ask, you know, you have to do what they want you to. Jimmy says cooperate: 'You know the media, if you're nice to them, they might be nice to you.'"

This is like a zoo, Lucille Kelley thought. She had regained consciousness in the emergency room of St. Vincent's Hospital in Greenwich Village. There was a woman next to her, vomiting on her. The room was filled with moans. She heard someone say: "Jimmy Carter's wife called about her."

Miss Kelley's skull was dented, but X rays showed no

fracture. It took 18 stitches to close the gash in the back of her head. "Can I have a private room?" she asked. "I don't want anyone to see me this way."

"Madam," said the doctor, "in New York a private room means eight beds."

Patrolmen Artie Stoecker and Mark Sultan of the NYPD Pimp Squad went off duty at midnight. They decided to go over to the French Quarter at the Americana to have a drink with the Morals team—Jim Gallagher's men—assigned to the bar. Walking along 53rd Street, they passed two women, white, not bad. "Looking for a date, honey?" one said.

Why not? "Sure," Stoecker said. "I know this is going to cost me." They agreed on $100 each. "What are you going to do for $100? A blow job?"

"We'll do anything you want," one of the women said.

The conversation was a ritual. To make an arrest, New York cops were required to discuss—or testify that they had discussed—a price and a specific sexual act. But the prostitutes knew what they were doing, too, and one of them "tossed" Stoecker—quickly embracing him and running her hands tenderly down his back and finding the handcuffs hung on his belt. "Wait a minute," the plainclothesman said, grabbing her as she started to run. "Take it easy, we're Jimmy Carter's security men. We're not even from New York."

"Yeah," she said, "where's he?"

"He's upstairs, on the 21st floor." For some reason, the women knew that was true and after some more talking, they agreed to go up there for "a little party." Stoecker, Sultan, and the two prostitutes walked into the hotel and took an elevator to the 16th floor. "You wait here," Stoecker said. "We'll go upstairs and make sure that the party's started and that things are cool. There'll be some important people there." The women giggled, and the two men got into an "Up" elevator.

"What do we do now?" Sultan said. "We're suppose to make friends with them, not bust them."

"I guess we have to get the pussy posse." They got off on the 18th floor and took another elevator down to the lobby and called headquarters. They were told to wait for Morals Squad men. Back to the 16th floor and Stoecker said: "We have to wait until things get started. Let's go down to the coffee shop."

In a few minutes, Angelo Parisi and Anthony Santiago of Gallagher's squad came into the shop and were introduced as two more Carter guards. By this time, everyone was friendly, kidding. Stoecker and Sultan said they were going up to the 21st floor, that they would meet everybody there. Parisi and Santiago went through the price-and-act conversation again. Then Parisi said: "I'm sorry, girls. We're police officers, and you're under arrest."

The two women began to cry. They later identified themselves as schoolteachers from Miami who did a little hustling on the side and thought there would be big money at the Convention.

At 2:00 A.M., George Dillman, a Texas banker who had volunteered to work on credentials distribution, was sitting in his Garden office unhappily counting rose-colored "Floor" passes. No matter how many times he tried, he came up 150 short for each of Wednesday and Thursday nights. He also could not account for the same number for the Tuesday session which ended two hours earlier. It seemed impossible, but someone had gotten into the locked and guarded office and walked out with 450 passes—there was going to be one hell of a lot of trouble if a floor fight developed and one side or another had the means to get 150 agents out among the delegations.

Jane O'Reilly, the columnist, was at a California delegation party at the New York Hilton in deep conversation with Carter's pollster, Pat Caddell, an encounter she recorded this way: "He told me a lot of inside stuff—which I later saw everywhere in the press."

Back at the Garden, eight men were meeting in the office of Jim Teague, the DNC's hall manager, about the fallen Iowa standard—how and why? "Meeting" was a polite word because there was a lot of shouting back and forth after their belt pages—beepers—went off summoning them as soon as Lucille Kelley was hit. Teague, Mickey McCauley of the Garden, Jeff Sommer of Mayor Beame's office, Ed Hurwitz of Office Design Associates, Charles Uribe of A-J Contracting, and the others were trying to figure out what to do. The sleeves holding the standards could not be bolted into the Garden floor without damaging the equipment that mixed 7,400 gallons of water and 250 gallons of white paint to lay a ⅝-inch layer of ice for hockey games.

Andy Shea, the Convention manager, came in shouting: "We have to stop this. We have to stop this. How could this happen?"

"You were the one who didn't want to bolt them to the chairs because it would take away from the excitement of the Convention."

At 3:00 A.M., again with her loyal friends, Clare Smith went to the Americana to try to find Hunter Thompson. With the others waiting down the hall, she knocked and someone said. "What?"

"Is Hunter there?"

"No."

"Bullshit!"

That brought the man himself to the door. Clare said she wanted his autograph. She was very scared because her hero was making growling noises and jumping from side to side in the doorway. She figured, though, that he didn't have glasses on and probably could not see her well. She pushed a white envelope into his hand, and he held it against the wall and scrawled: "H. S. Thompson, 7-14-76. NYC."

"Hunter, why aren't you writing *Fear and Loathing in 1976?*"

"Because of shit like this!" he shouted. "Now get out of here."

By 10:00 P.M., Annie was unhappily back on the "Meat Rack" on Delancey Street. She turned three tricks before 11:30—most of the competition was not in her class or age group—when a taxi pulled to the curb. The driver got out and asked whether she would spend the night with "a guy from the Convention and his daughter." "I think they just want to talk," the driver said. Two hundred dollars.

There was a man and a teenager in the cab, and Annie went with them to the Americana. For the rest of the night, the three of them talked. The girl, who said she was 16, began by asking: "When do you sleep?"

"Where is the best place to work?" the man asked.

"Park Avenue and 29th Street. The guys are nice and rich."

"Do you have a pimp?"

"No. I ran out on him. But he'll come gunning for me. I'm scared. He shot at me twice, and I went to the cops. There's an attempted-murder warrant out for him. But I'm gonna make it on my own if it kills me."

At 7:30 in the morning, the door to the adjacent room opened and a woman and young boy stepped in. "This is my wife and son, Annie," the man said, getting up. The five of them went downstairs for breakfast at the hotel's coffee shop.

Dick Celeste's postsession staff meeting was not as cheerful as usual. He had not gotten on television. He got to the microphone at 5:59, just as CBS and NBC were cutting away to their local stations. Instead of hearing Celeste call them into a "Constituency of Conscience," Americans were serenaded with commercials calling them to Ford's Torino and "All the Best," NBC's fall lineup of situation comedies.

At least he had been on the winning side. The minority report allowing issue debate—the report Celeste argued laboriously against—was defeated 1,950½ to 730½ as Jimmy Carter's floor captains passed their first test, walking the floor between delegations signaling thumbs-down. And Celeste had a negative triumph of sorts—his troops reported that his probable rival in Ohio's 1978 gubernatorial primary, Attorney General William Brown, got only 50 people to his welcoming cocktail party in New York. Besides, one of Brown's assistants had thrown out Gene Jordan of the *Columbus Dispatch,* one of the state's more important political columnists, telling Jordan it was a private party—"No press!"

But Celeste's national television debut would have to wait, perhaps for four years.

When Lynda Bird Robb left the VVIP section, she said to Mark Gasarch, the chief usher there, that she had been interviewed by all three networks. It was fun, she said. "We'll be back tomorrow."

Making conversation, Gasarch picked up on the "we," asking, "Will your sister be with you?"

"Luci's in Europe," Mrs. Robb replied. "But if she thought there was a chance to get on television, she'd fly right back."

☒ **Wednesday**

July 14

"**H**ave you heard anything about your priest?" Edward Bennett Williams, the party's treasurer, said to Robert Strauss in a midafternoon phone call on the third day of the Convention.

"My priest?" said Strauss, who grew up in the only Jewish family in Lockhart, Texas.

"Father Deming," Williams said—the Reverend Robert N. Deming, rector of the Cathedral of the Immaculate Conception in Kansas City, Missouri, who was scheduled to give the benediction at the end of that night's session. Williams, who was counsel to the National Catholic Council of Bishops, said that a friend at the council had called and told him Deming had been talking to his superior, the bishop of Kansas City, the Reverend Charles Helmsing, about the Democratic platform's opposition to a constitutional amendment banning abortions. "Deming may be thinking of skipping on you tonight," Williams said.

A headline flashed in Strauss's head. On the morning after Jimmy Carter was nominated at Bob Strauss's Convention, the front page of the *New York Daily News* would say:

CATHOLICS BOYCOTT
DEM CONVENTION

The chairman called in his assistant, Azie Morton, and Convention manager Andy Shea's assistant, Jackie Falk— the two women had become friendly with Father Deming during the Democrats' 1974 Mid-Term Conference in Kansas City and suggested that he be given a role at the Convention. Ms. Falk assured Strauss that things were fine, that she had seen Deming at his hotel, the Waldorf Astoria, and they had parted saying that they would see each other at Madison Square Garden when the night's session began at 8:00 P.M.

Twenty blocks uptown at the offices of the New York Host Committee, Mimi Gurbst was having trouble getting off the phone at all. On each of the first two days of the Convention, the committee had handled 150 requests for "Honored Guest" credentials. By noon, Ms. Gurbst had already received 500 requests for the night's nominating session. She also found out there was a way of deciding who got in and who did not: "It's the checkbook. Money controls everything. The rich ones made it, and it was 'sorry' for everybody else."

The push was on; no one would be outside the Garden giving out tickets tonight. Rima Parkhurst of the Democratic National Committee's credentials office was approached by 40 delegates who said that they had lost their credentials and needed another. "Okay," she said, "we'll give them to you and put your original numbers on the 'Hot List'; when the thief tries to get in the police will grab him." Figuring out what that meant, all 40 said they would not take new credentials, they would look for their old ones. Her favorite was a delegate who appeared with a heavily made-up woman, wearing a wig, hot pants, and thigh-high white boots. He said he had fainted the night before, and his doctor told him to bring a nurse—this was his nurse.

"You've got to be kidding," Ms. Parkhurst said.

"Won't work, huh?" he said.

Dorothy Schiff, the publisher of the *New York Post,* said she needed an extra pass for her chauffeur—that she never went anywhere without her chauffeur. Didn't work.

When Rima Parkhurst undressed for bed that night, she saw that her arms were black and blue from elbow to shoulder after a day of friendly arm-grabs from credential seekers.

The push was also on for Jimmy Carter's body—his presence. The Carter scheduling office on the 21st floor of the Americana, which already had 1,500 written Convention Week invitations for the candidate plus hundreds more, many not even opened, in Atlanta, was handling more than 100 more a day by telephone. Some were easy—they turned down the "Today" show because the candidate was not going to do any live television before the nomination, and they turned down the woman who called and said she must talk to "Jimmy" about the vision she just had; also, the woman in Brooklyn who said she had grits on the table and thought Carter might like to stop by.

The serious ones were divided among the family, and there was a lot of family to go around—in order of priority, Jimmy, Rosalynn, Miss Lillian, the children, brothers and sisters, even in-laws, cousins, nieces, and nephews. The New York delegation, the largest at the Convention and the host delegation, expected Jimmy for their 9:00 A.M. breakfast caucus in the Mercury Room of the New York Hilton. They got Dr. Robert Stapleton, a veterinarian from Fayetteville, North Carolina, who was married to the candidate's sister. Mrs. Stapleton, a traveling evangelist, did not come—she had flown to a booksellers' convention in

Atlantic City to promote her bestseller, *The Gift of Inner Healing*. At the Americana, the incident was tabbed "Scheduling's Revenge"—retribution for more than two dozen calls from Mary Beame, Mayor Beame's wife, insisting that Carter spend an afternoon sitting for a friend of hers who painted portraits.

If getting even was the name of the game, Abraham Beame defended the family honor by getting up to introduce Dr. Stapleton to the New York delegates and . . . and not being able to remember his name.

Things were not going so well at the Statler Hilton either. The main escalator broke down again, this time for 12 hours. Then, Sal Lividini, the manager, found out he was losing one of his main television attractions. Senator Walter Mondale, a vice-presidential possibility, checked out, and no one was quite sure why or where he had gone.

Outside, on Seventh Avenue, John Mastrion, a New York sanitationman, was sweeping debris from the gutter. His assignment for the Convention was eight square blocks, 30th to 34th Streets between Sixth and Eighth Avenues— about one-tenth the area he was usually expected to keep clean, and couldn't. "Hey, man!" a black pedestrian shouted angrily. "How come they never clean our streets this way? How come, man? How come we can't get that service on 125th Street in Harlem?"

Minorities might have trouble with garbage collection, but they could get the candidate. Jimmy Carter left his suite just after 11:30 A.M. to go downstairs for a short appearance before the Latino Caucus. He told his speechwriters that he would be back in 15 minutes. It is one of the traditional privileges of political rank that when the top guy arrives at any function, he is quickly introduced, says his piece, and then leaves to cheers and waving arms.

But the Latinos had several introducers on the program.

The first, David Amaba, a California Chicano leader, was still speaking at 11:55, demanding presidential pardons for "so-called illegal aliens working in the fields of California and the Southwest." Barely turning his head and speaking so softly that only Amaba and those near him could hear, Carter said: "You can keep talking if you wish, but I will leave."

Amaba sat down. But Herman Badillo, a Puerto Rican congressman from New York, took the microphone and began with a rhetorical question about the candidate's attitude toward Hispanic-American issues. Before Badillo could continue, Carter stood, said, "I'd like to answer that"—did his 10 minutes and started to leave. Badillo, who had lost his chance to speak, was quicker this time, holding onto the candidate as photographers moved in. Ramon Velez, a New York City councilman opposing Badillo in a congressional primary, saw that and rushed to Carter, threw his arms around the candidate, faced the photographers, and shouted: "Viva Carter! Viva Carter!" Carter smiled.

While Carter was downstairs, his friend Charlie Kirbo got a call from Mickey Kantor, Jerry Brown's campaign manager. "Let me think out loud with you," Kantor said. "If Governor Brown wanted to come to the Convention tonight and call for Carter's nomination by acclamation, what would happen?" Well, Kirbo said, he wasn't sure, he thought maybe Bob Strauss was working out something different, that Georgia wanted to make that motion for their native son.

The pimple, Kirbo reported later to Strauss, seemed to be about ready to pop.

Fritz Efaw, the draft evader who was about to announce that he was a candidate for vice-president, got a phone call after breakfast from Alex Knopp, a friend he had met in

London. "Please don't have Ramsey Clark do the nominating speech. It would hurt Bella," said Knopp, who now worked for Representative Bella Abzug, one of Clark's opponents in the New York senatorial primary. Then Knopp paused and laughed nervously, "Fritz? Look, she's making me do this."

A little later, two more Abzug assistants, Lee Novick and Mim Gelber, appeared at the offices of the National Council for Universal and Unconditional Amnesty, loudly protesting that Efaw's supporters were trying to destroy Ms. Abzug by giving Clark free television time. "I think it's quite sad," said Ms. Novick, the congresswoman's administrative assistant, "that after all these years of alliance in the peace movement you people can do this to Bella."

Efaw sat in a corner of the office, looking at the floor and softly repeating, "Shit. Shit. Shit . . ."

You can get from the Americana Hotel to Madison Square Garden in about five minutes for 50 cents—if you take the subway. Most delegates and convention visitors preferred to pay $2.00 for a taxi, taking the chance that the trip might take three times as long if they got caught in the traffic that backed up Seventh Avenue from 33rd Street.

The New York City subway system—708 noisy, grimy, fascinating miles—is one of the wonders of the world. It is also one of the most efficient and cheapest public transit networks on the planet, moving 3.5 million people each day at speeds up to 55 miles per hour. It does not, however, have what you would call a good public image. New York officials assured the Democratic National Committee that there would be no transportation problems at the Convention because of the subway and even suggested that volunteer guides, pretty girls in blue uniforms, might be provided for each train or even each car. "Won't they be raped?" asked a member of the Arrangements Committee. Inevitably, the city had to spend $200,000 for 120 buses to shuttle delegates between their hotels and the Garden.

Clare Smith was warned several times to stay away from the subway—"Never the subway!"—so she took it back from the Staten Island Ferry on Sunday after her first adventure in New York, a trip into the harbor to see the Statue of Liberty. On the way, her friend Dottie Sievers said, "Turn around, you can tell we're really in New York." There was a man standing against a wall with his pants down around his ankles.

Jack and Joan Haines lived on a farm near Chardon, Ohio, and when Mrs. Haines was elected as a delegate, they decided this was the time for their children to see how the other half lived. For three days in New York they walked and took taxis to see the city with their 15-year-old son John and their 10-year-old twins, Jason and Lauren. On Wednesday afternoon, they decided to take the subway from the Sheraton to Madison Square Garden. They were directed to an entrance just outside the hotel at 55th Street and Seventh Avenue.

Two levels below the ground they stepped into a waiting car. "Will this take us to Madison Square Garden?" Jack asked. "No. This is the Uptown. Take any train across the platform."

They hustled out of the car as the doors snapped shut. It was a moment before Mrs. Haines realized that Lauren hadn't made it. Her daughter's face was in the moving window, her hands banging the dirty glass. Her twin, Jason, ran wildly along with the train, trying to pull the doors open until his father caught him, lifting him back.

Joan Haines stood terrified while her husband raced away, looking for a dispatcher, anyone in authority. "There is nothing you can do," a black woman said to Mrs. Haines. "You can't leave because someone might send her back here. I'll get on the next train and check every station to Queens. What's her name?"

On the train, Lauren was sobbing and passengers told her to get off at the next station and wait. She did get off and sat on a bench. When the next train clattered in, a black woman got off and walked directly to her: "Is your name Lauren Haines?"

The woman and Lauren, hand in hand, were back at 55th Street within ten minutes. Joan Haines broke into tears, embracing the woman and then her daughter, then turning to say, "We don't even know your name . . ." The woman was gone.

At Carter press headquarters in the Americana, Kevin Gorman announced to a hundred dull-eyed reporters that there would be an announcement at 2:15 P.M. Pencils rose to the ready. "Dan Mitchell, one of the stars of 'Ironside' and his wife, Judy Pace, will be here for an endorsement and brief press conference."

"What's 'Ironside'?"

"It used to be a television show."

"Who's Don Mitchell?"

"Dan. It's Dan. He was the guy who pushed Raymond Burr's wheelchair. He's black."

Gorman, an assistant press secretary, stepped down from the little stage in the pressroom and was grabbed by a woman holding up a canvas tote bag with an imprint of the front page of the *New York Daily News* displaying the grim headline: PAT NIXON SUFFERS STROKE.

"We're selling these for seven dollars," said the woman, who was named Elle Kofler. "Can you get us a pretty delegate to pose with one of these?"

"But . . ." Gorman started to say.

"It won't be this headline," Ms. Kofler said. "It will be the headline when Carter is nominated."

Oh! The Carter staff had set up a whole ballroom—Albert Hall, off the Americana's lobby—to handle people like Elle Kofler. It was a phony campaign headquarters described in an internal memo as "A 'zoo' area, where the public could feel inside the campaign while really being outside."

Albert Hall was complete with doors impressively marked with signs like "Campaign Manager—Hamilton Jordan" and a desk that said "Polling—Pat Cadell." The thought was there, even if Caddell's name was misspelled and chairs were filled by volunteers and the lowest-level staff people—the volunteers, of course, did not know they were being used as public-fodder—and even if one desk-filler did try to beat up two of the people he was supposed to be interviewing. The idea was to channel the hustlers, the nuts, and real but unneeded volunteers into Albert Hall and away from the real business of the campaign—and, in fact, 400 legitimate "Carter Volunteers" were signed up by other volunteers each day. "There were thousands of people coming to the Americana every day, a lot of them wanting to talk to Carter or to take over from Charlie Kirbo," said Jim Gammill, the candidate's Convention coordinator. "We had to put them someplace, and Albert Hall was someplace."

The real Hamilton Jordan was 30 floors above Albert Hall meeting with officials of the American Federation of Labor–Congress of Industrial Organizations. "Do you want a unified labor effort or a factional one?" asked Lane Kirkland, the number two man in the AFL-CIO, which had been generally hostile to the Carter candidacy from the beginning.

"That's not a hard question," answered Jordan with a smile. What was going on was more trading of the power that Hurley Goodall and other dedicated local workers had won for Jimmy Carter. First, Goodall's delegate seat from Munice, Indiana, had been traded to the Indiana Coalition in return for the support of the eight liberal Labor Coalition unions in later primaries. Now, the coalition's influence was going to be turned over to the bigger AFL-CIO and its president, George Meany.*

Kirkland said that the AFL-CIO objected to the Carter campaign's plans to use a Coalition representative as a labor spokesman and Jordan said the plan would be dropped. Alexander Barkan, director of the AFL-CIO's Committee on Political Education, said that COPE could organize 18 million members and their families; that in 1968 it distributed 55 million pieces of literature for Hubert Humphrey—*but* that those efforts and that organization could be diverted from the presidential campaign to congressional campaigns.

"Our lines are open," Kirkland said. "George Meany will return Governor Carter's calls; you and I can talk. We have a regional office in Atlanta; we can strengthen that."

Jordan smiled and said, "This would be another step in our educational process."

"The roll call for president is tonight, and you know what that means if the sound is no good," Steve Alper of the network Pool said to Mickey McCauley, Madison

---

* The ILC was part of the Labor Coalition Clearinghouse (the "Coalition"), whose members included the National Education Association, United Auto Workers, United Mine Workers, International Association of Machinists, Communication Workers of America, and American Federation of State, County, and Municipal Workers. The Coalition made a determined effort to exert as much control as possible over the Democratic National Convention. In New York, 582 delegates were union members, 418 from Coalition unions, 172 of them from NEA, the teachers' union, alone. But, although some Coalition unions were also AFL-CIO affiliates, the Coalition was considered something of a rival by George Meany and other AFL-CIO leaders.

Square Garden's Convention coordinator. "We're going to bypass the Garden system. I don't care what happens. We're going to do it."

The Pool controlled the delegation microphones on the floor, but their sound passed into the Garden's—and Norman Leonard's—amplifiers before coming out of the loudspeakers. And so far, what had come through those amplifiers had not been very clear. The Garden blamed acoustics altered by Convention construction, poor planning by the Democratic National Committee, and Pool equipment; the Pool blamed Norman Leonard and his union, the IBEW. And the Pool was afraid they would be embarrassed or blamed if it was difficult to hear delegation leaders announce their presidential votes. That was the reason for the "emergency" bypass cable laid by the network people during the pre-Convention struggles between network and Garden personnel.

Alper and a crew of eight men headed for the rooms under the podium. The Pool manager ordered his technicians to plug in the cable—eliminating any role for Leonard's people or equipment—while three Garden electricians stood over the connection. Leonard, a former boxer with a reputation of being a very tough guy, came into the room at that moment and came toward Alper.

"Hold it," one of the men with Alper said. "We don't want any trouble here, do we?" It was Sergeant Porter of Manhattan Homicide. Alper had come with two cops and two Secret Service agents dressed as workmen.

Jim Dugan polled the New Jersey delegation for the first time at 3:30 in the Jade Room. He had talked too much —even if it had been off the record, and too many Jersey newspapers had reported that "delegation leaders" were saying the state was going unanimously for Carter. And too many delegates had then given interviews saying that was not true, that they were not giving their votes to the man they ran against. "I think we, uh, I've got a little work to do in the Thirty-seventh District," Dugan said, glaring at Michael Cohan, a delegate from Englewood who said "Brown" during the roll call.

A dozen others said "Brown," or "Humphrey," or "Uncommitted." Assemblyman Francis Gorman of Gloucester City, who had returned to the state capital, Trenton, for the day, telephoned in "Brown," leaving a note for Dugan that he had promised his ten children he would vote for the Californian. Francine Rein of Bloomfield, who was elected in the Twenty-seventh District campaigning for Brown, said "Uncommitted."

Dugan was short at least 15 votes of the unanimous package he had wanted to deliver to Jimmy Carter in return for control of the presidential campaign in New Jersey. That was the deal. The state chairman and his lieutenants told Jersey reporters—off the record—not to take the roll call too seriously. A lot of these people were just holding out to get extra credentials for the last two sessions. "Most of these delegates could not care less about who is going to be nominated. What they want is a ticket so that their wife or girlfriend can get into the Garden," was a quotation the *New York Times* attributed to "one delegation official."

Francine Rein, wearing her "Brown" button, walked out of the caucus in confusion. One of the reasons she did not want to vote for Carter was that the Georgian was supported by Essex County Democratic Chairman Harry Lerner, and she had spent five years fighting Lerner—a do-good housewife after the county "boss." Now the pressure was on: William Brach, of Montclair, her running mate in the primary, told her that a vote for Brown was actually a vote for Lerner because if Dugan did not deliver a united delegation, the Carter people might turn over the county campaign to Lerner. That's the way politics is in Jersey. Mrs. Rein broke into tears and went upstairs to her room.

Inside the empty room, Fran Rein said: "Fuck this scene."

"Well, Mr. Chairman," said Robert Gafford of Birmingham at the 5:00 P.M. caucus of the Alabama delegation, "when you order chicken and get possum, it takes a little while to get used to. I'm voting for George Wallace."

He was booed. By the Alabama delegation! The party's state chairman, Robert Vance, the delegation chairman, Bob Wilson, and Wallace's young political strategist, Mickey Griffin, had all stood before the 35 delegates at the New York Hilton and said the governor would be "embarrassed" if his state did not cast all 35 votes for Jimmy Carter when the presidential roll was called that night.

Larry Morris was next—"I was swallowing hard"—and he began, "I do not feel in good faith that I can vote for Jimmy Carter . . ." He was cut off by boos and angry shouts from some of the strongest Wallace supporters he knew, from friends. So this was unity? Yeller Dawg Democrats, Morris thought, that's what they used to call the old straight-ticket voters in Alabama—they'd vote Democratic even if there was a yellow dog on the ticket.

Dick Celeste's big party was scheduled from 5:00 to 7:00 P.M. in the large Sheraton suite of the Ohio state chairman, Paul Tipps. At the last minute Celeste got nervous and told his assistant, Jerry Austin, that he needed something extra to make sure that people would remember the party. Austin went to a wholesale house at Sixth Avenue and 42nd Street and spent $60 for a 100-pound bag of peanuts. "This is the fourth bag I've sold this way in three days," said the man behind the counter. "What's going on?"

By 6:00 P.M., 300 people had showed up, and many had to stand in the hallways. That was great, but what was better was that Celeste and John Glenn got a chance to talk for a while—Celeste badly wanted the former astronaut's help in two years. Glenn said that he was glad Celeste had been careful not to push too openly for him for vice-president. Carter, Glenn was sure, would have been offended. Celeste did not tell him that he had brought 10,000 old Glenn campaign buttons to New York and had been undecided about whether to pass them around. A Glenn candidacy would help any politician in Ohio—it would also open up a United States Senate seat and, at the least, Celeste would be a likely candidate.

The Celestes, lieutenant governor, wife, and father— Frank Celeste was paying for some of his son's activities, including suite 2018—headed for Madison Square Garden and the presidential balloting. Austin stayed to clean up the mess, clogging two vacuum cleaners with peanut shells before the hotel provided an industrial vacuum.

It was almost six o'clock when Clare Smith got to the Garden. She had slept until noon and then joined a "Christmas shopping" excursion organized by Alan Rapoport, another young Carter delegate. He wanted to buy crystal and said there were great buys at Tiffany's. The first item they saw after finding the store on Fifth Avenue was a necklace priced at $4,000.

"Where is the budget floor?" Alan asked.

"At Tiffany's, there is no budget floor, sir."

As she went to her seat on the floor, Clare was stopped

by Rick Weber, the good-looking page. He handed her a bottle of cologne, gift-wrapped from Bergdorf Goodman.

In the Texas delegation, Jeff Jones, a delegate from that state, and Peter Galbraith, John Kenneth's son, were collecting signatures on a vice-presidential petition for Louise Ransom, a director of the National Council for Universal and Unconditional Amnesty whose son had been killed in action in Vietnam. The Ransom petitions were a back-up for Fritz Efaw's. If Chairman Strauss ruled Efaw's nomination out of order because of his age, Mrs. Ransom would be nominated, getting the same 15 minutes of television.

Across the street at the Statler Hilton, Representative John Conyers of Michigan was doing the same thing for his friend, Representative Ronald Dellums of California, whose symbolic nomination was being pushed by some liberals and Black Caucus members who wanted to remind Jimmy Carter that they were still alive.

The congressman figured that he could collect most of the 50 delegate signatures at the cocktail party of Americans for Democratic Action, for years the institutionalized voice of Democratic liberals. "There is no spokesman for the left this year, except for Dellums," he announced at the ADA party. "Would the delegates here please step up?" There were only three delegates in the room.

In room 1930 of the Americana, Dr. Milton Bryant, an Atlanta surgeon, was injecting pain-killers into Charles Neuenschwander, a Secret Service agent assigned to Carter who had torn the muscles in his left shoulder tripping down a flight of stairs. The agent was one of more than 400 people treated during the week by the doctor, who had paid his own way to the Convention to serve as the Carter staff physician, using $3,000 worth of drugs donated by the Robbins Company of Richmond, Virginia. His records portrayed the Carter staff as nondrinking, calm folks who were not used to New York—not a single hangover complaint, only a half-dozen prescriptions for Valium, but almost 100 cases he recorded as "Montezuma's Revenge," people whose intestinal systems could not handle New York drinking water.

Bob Strauss was in his office at the Statler Hilton when he got the call from Azie Morton. "You better get right over here," she said. She was crying.

Father Deming, the Kansas City priest, was with Mrs. Morton in Strauss's dressing room office behind the podium. Ed Williams had been right. The priest had a letter saying that he could not give the benediction that night "as a matter of conscience."

"Who's making you do this?" said Strauss, who was convinced that the 42-year-old priest was being pressured by the Council of Bishops, which was already on record as opposing the Democratic platform's abortion plank. Father Deming said that he did not want to discuss his reasons, that it was a personal matter.

Azie Morton and Jackie Falk were crying in the corner of the room. Ed Williams came in at one point and for a while the priest, who said very little, was confronted by two of the most persuasive men in the country.

"Would you pray for a rapist who was a murderer if he was dying? Strauss asked.

"Yes."

"Are you telling me that a rapist and murderer is better than the Democratic party? Pray for us. That's all we're asking. You can denounce us," the chairman continued. "The podium's yours for as long as you want it. You act as if your only options are to support our platform or to cut and run. You can do whatever you want to do.

"If you cut and run and if there's a bad story, you could affect this campaign and possibly the future of this country. Is that what you want to do?"

It went on for more than an hour. Finally, Strauss had to go outside to open the third session of the Convention. "Don't make a mistake like this," he said, fairly sure that he had convinced Father Deming. "Promise me one thing, that before you make a final decision, you'll let me know."

"We fully recognize the religious and ethical nature of the concerns which many Americans have on the subject of abortion," began the platform plank that offended Father Deming. "We feel, however, that it is undesirable to attempt to amend the U.S. Constitution to overturn the Supreme Court decision in this area."

The plank had been adopted by an 8-to-4 vote of the Platform Committee in Washington on July 1. The vote superseded an earlier decision to avoid any mention at all of the controversial issue. Many of the people involved in changing the vote—and getting a proabortion statement into the platform—gave credit for the switch to one person, Mrs. Stuart Eizenstat, the wife of Jimmy Carter's representative at the platform hearings. After the first vote, Olay Margolin, a legislative representative for the National Council of Jewish Women, had telephoned Fran Eizenstat in Atlanta and asked her to talk with her husband about the strong feeling of many Democratic women that the issue should not be avoided. When Eizenstat called home that night, his wife began, "Stu, I cannot believe you are doing this . . ." The next morning, Eizenstat, the most influential arbiter of platform language, argued for reinstatement of the vaguely proabortion stance—and, as on virtually every other issue, the Carter arguments became platform language.

As Strauss mounted the podium, NBC was televising an interview with Father Robert Drinan, a Massachusetts congressman who was a Roman Catholic priest, a Jesuit. He was saying that the Democrats did have some problems with Catholic voters in his area, not so much because of abortion, but because they were "perplexed" by Jimmy Carter's evangelical style of Christianity. "It's a communications gap," Drinan said. "They don't understand a southern gentleman who talks about a second birth." Whatever it was, there was great concern about it within the Carter campaign. More than 29 million American Catholics were registered to vote—70 per cent of them in 12 large states with enough electoral votes (271) to choose a president—and Catholic voters normally go Democratic by about two-to-one. But not always—Richard Nixon carried a majority of Catholic voters against George McGovern in 1972. Carter obviously did not want a repeat, and he did not want to have a mirror image of the problem that John F. Kennedy faced in 1960 when many Protestant voters found his Catholicism cause for fear.

By 8:30, the crowd outside the main entrance of the Garden was pressing toward the event in the way that only New York crowds can press—the trick was to move forward sideways, using a shoulder, and pretending to reach for something or somebody ahead. Gordon Stewart, a tall, thin, and perpetually distracted playwright and director who dabbled in politics, was, in fact, trying to reach someone. He was rearranging pages in a file folder as he moved toward Margaret Costanza. "Midge" Costanza, the vice-mayor of Rochester, New York, was 5-foot-1, so she could get lost in a crowd, but she could also handle herself in one. The daughter of an Italian sausage maker and a secretary most of her life, she had been the first public official in New York to endorse the presidential ambitions of Jimmy Carter. She was trying to get inside to give one of the two seconding speeches for his nomination, and the speech, written by Stewart, was inside the folder—except page 5 was soon blowing down Seventh Avenue, chased by Stewart. "Please keep moving," a cop said, moving Stewart away. Midge Costanza snatched the folder from Stewart and plunged in.

Inside, Clare Smith was doing what she worked six months to do. An Ohio whip looked down the 12th row of the state delegation and asked Clare, "Carter?"

"Yeah," she said. He made a mark on a green sheet. One vote for Jimmy Carter from Ohio—one of the 1,505 he needed for the Democratic nomination for president of the United States.

Rick Weber came over to Clare again and asked whether she wanted to go with him to a really good bar the next night. Yes.

Twenty blocks uptown, on the 21st floor of the Americana, Clare's grouchy hero, Hunter Thompson, was sitting in the office of Carter's press secretary, Jody Powell, waiting to get some time with the candidate. The phone rang— a CBS producer wanted to confirm a rumor that Carter was planning to come downstairs to a ballroom to speak to his troops after the nomination roll call.

"I don't know if we can stop him," Thompson told CBS. "We hope we can, but Jimmy's so drunk we may not be able to."

The great vice-president hunt was turning into hide-and-seek. The three apparent front-runners for Carter's blessing had all concluded that the Georgian was a man who did not like to be pushed, so they all decided to disappear— or try to, anyway. After his checkout at the Statler Hilton, Senator Walter Mondale canceled all his scheduled public appearances and his staff issued a statement saying he was "at a location somewhere in the city." He was in a $500-a-day penthouse suite at the elegant Carlyle Hotel on East 80th Street, where he had been sleeping all along, preferring it to the faded glory of the Statler, where he had worked —given interviews—during the day. The ploy worked well enough that his home-state paper, the *Minneapolis Tribune,* was headlining: MONDALE IN SECLUSION AS SUSPENSE MOUNTS.

Senator Edmund Muskie was trying to hide in even more artistic surroundings. His staff told the press that the senator and his wife would be visiting the Metropolitan Museum of Art. Actually, they planned to go to the Whitney Museum of American Art—alone, they hoped. But reporters spotted the Muskies getting into a station wagon outside the Gotham Hotel—"Follow that cab!" Two cabloads of reporters and an ABC camera van trailed the Muskies to the Whitney, running red lights to keep up.

Senator John Glenn and his wife went to dinner together in the Sky Club, one of New York's many panoramic restaurants, this one on top of the 57-story Pan Am building which overlooked the city from Park Avenue and 44th Street. The senator's press secretary, Steve Avakian, had been assigned to sit by the $229 telephone, just in case.

The phone rang at 9:30. It was Carter's assistant, Greg Schneiders, telling him that *the* call would come at about 8:30 in the morning, could someone be there to take it? Avakian thought that could be arranged. Carter had told Schneiders that he would be up at 6:00 A.M.—he wanted to try parts of the acceptance speech on a tape recorder— and that he would notify the seven vice-presidential finalists an hour-and-a-half before a scheduled 10:00 A.M. unveiling news conference, because the Secret Service needed that much time to place guards around the man chosen.

"Will you yell the name to us on the way to the press

conference," asked Pat Caddell, "or do we find out along with the press?"

"Everybody finds out with the press," Carter said.

Fritz Efaw was on the floor again, looking for a nominator to place his name before the Convention as a candidate for vice-president. He had given in to the continuing pressure from Bella Abzug and her friends and told Ramsey Clark that he just could not accept his offer. Now Efaw wanted to find Governor Milton Shapp of Pennsylvania, the nominator proposed by Ms. Abzug.

"I'd be glad to help," Shapp said. "I'll second your nomination proudly. But I won't give the first speech."

The American politician: Second in war, second in peace, second in the hearts of his countrymen. Efaw stared at Shapp, but could not mouth the words in his mind: Fuck you. It's people like you who got us into the war and drove me out of the country. Fuck all of you. Fuck politics.

But when he spoke, his voice was controlled and, he hoped, cold: "Well, if that's the best you can do, that's the best you can do."

Efaw decided then that no matter who pushed him anymore, there were going to be no "name" Democrats using his name on the podium. He was going to ask Louise Ransom to be the nominator and Ron Kovic to do the seconding. Kovic, whom Efaw had met at the *Rolling Stone* party, was a 30-year-old former Marine sergeant who had been wounded in Vietnam in 1968 and paralyzed from the chest down, and then become a conspicuous symbol of Vietnam Veterans Against the War. Confined to a wheelchair, he was at the Convention to promote amnesty and his book, *Born on the Fourth of July*. No one knew exactly what to make of Kovic, who drew attention to himself and his plight wherever he went—especially the folks at the New York Hilton, who sent an assistant manager to Kovic's room each morning at 9:00 A.M. to collect the day's rent, $48, in advance. After the first day's $48 was paid in cash, though, the hotel agreed to cash Kovics's Veterans Administration disability check.

The rules of the VIP game changed Wednesday night. Whether it was the lure of the presidential balloting or the pace-setting of Jackie O., people no longer wanted to say they could be there if they wanted to—they wanted to. But now there was a third test to get into Sections 56, 57, and 58: "Honored Guest" credentials, plus the blue VVIP card, plus your name on a list held by Mark Gasarch. There were 76 names on the list—each one approved by Rosalynn Carter or Helen Strauss.

Phyllis Cerf Wagner, the wife of former New York Mayor Robert F. Wagner, was not one of the 76. She tried to sit in the third row, where she had sat for the first two nights, next to her friend Mary Beame, the wife of the current mayor. Mark Gasarch said there had been some changes and asked her to sit in the sixth row—in one of 12 seats he had roped off to handle problems like this.

"I want my usual seat," she said.

"It's been reserved," he said.

"For whom?"

"For Senator Humphrey."

"I'll take the next one."

"It's reserved for Senator McGovern." Gasarch was making up the names, but he figured Mrs. Wagner would run out of empty seats before he ran out of senators. Things were getting tense.

"I'm tired of being pushed around," she said. "What is your name?"

"Look, lady, will you sit down? I can fill this place with

the third wives of ex-mayors": that's what Gasarch thought
—and what he wanted to say. But he did say, "Please,
Mrs. Cerf, I . . ."

"The name," she said slowly, "is *Wag-ner.*" She had won.
She took the seat in the sixth row while Gasarch apologized
and apologized again for using the name of her late husband, publisher Bennett Cerf.

It was a long night. Mark Gasarch, who volunteered as
an aide because he wanted to see from the inside how things
worked, was finding out. Lee Radziwill came, Telly Savalas
came—their names were not on the list, and he had used
up his 12 discretionary seats. He got them into a couple of
empty seats in the Texas "Alternate" section next to VVIP
world—when the last alternates arrived, other Texans forcibly talked them out of unseating "The *Princess* Radziwill,
Jackie's sister" and "Kojak." But Punch Sulzberger of the
New York Times was turned away and so was Senator
Gary Hart of Colorado, who four years before, as Senator
McGovern's campaign manager, had been one of the men
that the Convention revolved around. Senator Humphrey
did come and there was trouble finding him a seat. NBC
correspondent Tom Brokaw, who wanted to get in to interview Mrs. Carter, got into a shoving match with a guard
named Arnie Markel. "Come and get me, big shot!" said
Markel, a laid-off New York cop. Brokaw lunged and was
held back by his camera crew as he yelled, "I won't forget
you, you creep"—which presumably meant that Markel
would never be on the "Today" show when Brokaw took
over as its new host after the Convention. One aide, Norman Raidow, a student at the State University of New
York, was dispatched to handle a woman of about 60
wearing a "Guest" tag, but seated in the Florida "Alternate"
section. "Excuse me, ma'am," Raidow said, "you're not
allowed in this seat and . . ." She punched him in the
mouth.

Gasarch told his troubles to his new friend, Rick Strauss, the son of the chairman. Young Strauss said he was surprised about the trouble with Mrs. Wagner because he had been to dinner at the Wagners' the night before and her matchbooks were monogrammed with *C* for Cerf.

"Can you get me one of those matchbooks?" Gasarch asked.

While Hunter Thompson was putting on CBS, and Phyllis Cerf was putting down Mark Gasarch, Edward Bennett Williams and Andy Shea were searching hotels and restaurants for Father Deming. They had no luck and just before ten o'clock, Williams went onto the Convention floor looking for Congressman Drinan, the Jesuit priest from Massachusetts.

Chairman Strauss decided to call Jimmy Carter, who was watching the Convention on television in his Americana suite. "We could get a very, very bad story out of this," he said. Carter told him not to worry, all he could do was his best.

"We may need a priest," Williams told Drinan.

"Well, I have a friend who teaches at Xavier High School. That's near here someplace, but it's summertime," Father Drinan said. He went behind the podium with Williams, looking for a telephone. His friend, in fact, was not there, said the priest who answered the phone in the rectory on East 23rd Street, Leo Daley.

America's most prominent Catholic politician, Teddy Kennedy, was making his one Convention appearance— not on the podium, but in the CBS anchor booth with Walter Cronkite. Asked about the goings-on, Senator Kennedy coolly avoided the presidential contest and began, "I'm obviously interested in being returned to the U.S. Senate . . ."

He said he admired Jimmy Carter's political skill and wished him well, but that he was going to be too busy campaigning for his own reelection to leave the state of Massachusetts. "But . . ." Cronkite fumbled for a way to ask Kennedy if he was disappointed, couldn't that be him being nominated out there tonight?

"You don't have to be a president of the United States to make a difference in this country," Kennedy said. "You don't even have to be a congressman. You make a difference, Mr. Cronkite."

Two levels below the CBS booth, one of Mr. Kennedy's former assistants, James King, was in the Carter delegate-communication trailer checking the telephones for taps. The candidate's 22-year-old convention coordinator, Jim Gammill, was convinced that someone was listening in on phone calls from the trailer—and he was sure that someone was Mr. Cronkite's network, CBS.

Jim King, whose hobby was electronics, had connected with the Carter campaign not because of his Kennedy experience but because he had been one of Gammill's instructors at Harvard's Kennedy Institute of Public Affairs. King checked the three outside phones in the trailer and said: "There's a power drop on each one. That could mean three things: one, an extension on the line and there are no extensions; two, a simple tap; three, some kind of general power drop in the Garden, which coincidentally happens every time I test a phone."

"Then they're bugged," said Gammill, the self-described paranoiac about the dirty tricks of networks and opponents.

"I didn't say that," King said. "But remember what I told you at the beginning, a telephone is just another electronic instrument, a microphone, and these lines are exposed to anyone walking around the Garden. Don't say anything in here that you don't want quoted on the front page of the *New York Times* or on CBS.

"Jim," King added, "it's inconceivable to me that a network would take that kind of chance."

It was not inconceivable to Gammill. He had called in his old instructor because he was convinced that CBS knew about a call made from the trailer a half-hour before by Zane Tankel, the New York printer who had the job of making 15,000 buttons and 4,000 posters with the names of both Jimmy Carter and his vice-presidential running mate.

Tankel had called the night foreman at his plant, Collier Lithography, and said, "We ready to go with all six?"

"No. We've only got Mondale. The rest are in rough comp."

"You've got to make them all," Tankel said. "We can't take the chance. We've got to be ready for whatever happens."

As he stepped outside the trailer a few minutes later, Tankel was stopped by Linda Ellerbee, an NBC correspondent who said, "I hear it's Mondale for vice-president, that he's the only one you're ready to print."

"That's impossible," Tankel said. "How do you know that? I just found out myself. But it's a mistake . . ." Ms. Ellerbee said that she had overheard a CBS producer saying that his network knew about the printing plans.

"Jim!" Tankel said, running toward Gammill. He lowered his voice: "Your phones are bugged."

By the luck of a draw held that afternoon, Jimmy Carter was the first candidate nominated for president. "With honest talk and plain talk," said Peter Rodino, "Jimmy Carter has appealed to the American people. . . . As he has brought a united South back into the Democratic party, he will bring a united Democratic party back into the leadership of America and a united America back to a position of respect and esteem in the eyes of the world."

Ellen McCormack, a housewife from Long Island who had collected 238,862 votes in 17 primaries and $234,-728.45 in Federal Election Commission matching funds as an antiabortion candidate, was nominated by James Killilea, a Massachusetts delegate, as she watched on television in a two-room suite at the Statler Hilton. With her was just about her entire campaign staff—her husband, John, a deputy inspector in the New York Police Department; John Mawn, a bus driver; and three other housewives. "There isn't a professional politician in this group," Mawn said, "but in a few years we'll be running the country."

Morris Udall was nominated by Archibald Cox, a Harvard professor who had become a hero to much of the nation when he was fired by President Richard Nixon as the special prosecutor investigating Watergate. Udall then took advantage of the Convention rules to get his message on television by seconding his own nomination. It was a witty, gracious speech, bringing tears to the eyes of many delegates who had worked for him for more than a year, and offering Jimmy Carter more comfort than Udall felt: "This is a good man. When he says he'll beat you, he beats you fair and square." On the 21st floor of the Americana, Jody Powell came out of Carter's suite, asking, "Where's Greg? Jimmy wants to call Mo."

Udall then formally withdrew his name from nomination. Jerry Brown, however, was not going to do that—there was something of a contest between the Brown and Udall staffs over who was going to finish second. The man who was going to nominate the Californian quieted the delegates— Cesar Chavez, the leader of the United Farm Workers, was a romantic curiosity, a small legend in the East.

Being a floor leader for Jimmy Carter had been a nice way for Frank Mankiewicz to wander the floor talking with old friends. He was responsible for the California and Texas delegations, among others, but there was not much to be responsible about—no fights. It was different from 1972, when Mankiewicz had been one of George McGovern's managers and watched the Convention slide into chaos, leaving McGovern a candidate without a party.

"Frank," said Diane Feinstein, a San Francisco County supervisor and Carter delegate, "we have to do something. The Brown people are mad as hell. Jerry offered to withdraw and move to make the nomination unanimous, but Carter has turned him down."

"That doesn't make sense," Mankiewicz said, "but I'll check it out." He went to the Carter trailers and found Hamilton Jordan, who said, "That's not true. I don't know anything about it and, if anybody was talking to Jerry Brown, I'd know about it."

Mankiewicz went back to the floor and told Ms. Feinstein it never happened. "It happened," said Leo McCarthy, the Speaker of the California Assembly and a Brown delegate. "Ask Mickey."

Mickey Kantor, Brown's manager, said it not only happened but that Brown himself was just on CBS saying he had been turned down. One of the functions of the networks at conventions has become to provide an internal communications system—television is the drums, the grapevine, the word. And the word was out; now things were serious. Mankiewicz and Kantor headed for the Carter trailer, grabbing Senator Alan Cranston as they went. In the trailer they sat down with Jordan—who by then knew that he hadn't known about Kirbo's negotiations—and worked out a plan: Brown would be nominated and after the roll call was completed, he would announce the first switch of the state votes, standing at the California microphone. Kantor telephoned Brown and the governor said he would think about it, but that he still wanted to go to the podium. Brown said he'd call right back.

They waited—more than an hour. Brown called back after ten o'clock, as Cesar Chavez was nominating him for president, and said he would do it—if Chairman Strauss agreed to recognize him from the podium. Cranston found Strauss behind the podium and told him what had happened. "Fine," the chairman said, "that's fine. I was just waiting to see what Jerry wanted to do."

Chavez was still speaking when Fran Rein, one of New Jersey's Brown delegates, got to the floor. The first person she met was Bernard Herrold, who had voted for Hubert Humphrey in the afternoon caucus. He said he was going to vote for Carter, that Humphrey himself had called him an hour ago and asked him to do it. "You better get on board," Herrold said. She noticed that Renee Dugan, the state chairman's wife, was sitting next to Sister Lucille Ann Egan, patting the nun's hand. Sister Lucille, a delegate from Convent Station in Morris County, had been a Brown holdout. They must have gotten to her, too.

When Chavez finished, CBS cut away to a commercial for Gallo wine, which Chavez's supporters had been boycotting since the winery canceled a UFW contract. Ken Babb and Cecil Porter were fighting their way through the aisles from the North Carolina delegation to the camera platform facing the podium. They had a bottle of vodka and some orange soda hidden under the platform—it was the only place in the Garden that non-VIPs could get a drink. But not all VIPs drank, either: each night Garden janitors swept up litters of marijuana butts in Sections 56 and 57.

Fran Rein burst into tears for the second time in six

hours when Richard Van Wagner, another Brown delegate, told her, "I hear Jerry is pulling out and releasing his delegates." She went off the floor with Mike Cohan, the Brown delegate Dugan thought needed some work, and they stood by Brown's command trailer, like two troops without a commander. Finally, they decided to talk to Jim Dugan.

"I resent the pressure being put on me," Mrs. Rein said to Dugan as he offered a handkerchief for her tears. "What am I doing, going from one boss to another? . . . Are we the last two?"

"You're among the last," Dugan said. "It will go very badly for New Jersey if we're not unanimous. Jimmy Carter is going to be president."

"Okay," she sighed. "You've got my vote."

"You know," said Mike Cohan, "Carter is alienated from the problems of the city and, let's face it, New Jersey's just one big city. I don't know. Maybe you're right. Maybe Carter will appreciate this and do something for us. You've got my vote, too."

Ann Compton of ABC was interviewing and being interviewed. A reporter from *Newsweek*'s "News Media" section came up to ask her: What did the reporter from *Time*'s "Press" section just ask you? Ms. Compton was holding Hugh Carter, the candidate's cousin, for her own interview, but the ABC control room kept going somewhere else. Finally they cut to Compton-Carter, but there was no Carter—cousin Hugh had been pulled away by Cassie Mackin of NBC and he was telling the competition's viewers what he thought was going on. Ms. Compton faked it, doing a short soliloquy on the Carter campaign, then took Hugh Carter by the hand and waited for her next cue. It never came.

The Pimp Squad cruiser, Patrolman Richie Confort's

own 1965 Cadillac, turned onto Park Avenue at 34th Street at 10:30. "Look at that," said Sergeant George Trapp. "That is one high-class hooker with the little guy. A hundred, two hundred dollars."

For four blocks, the car followed the couple—the woman was flashily dressed and seemed to be over six feet tall. At 38th Street, the couple crossed Park, right in front of Confort's car. "Oh, Jesus. You know who that is? That's Margaux Hemingway."

"Who?"

"Margaux Hemingway. She's no hooker. She's a big model, makes millions. The guy must be her husband. He's in hamburgers. You know the Wetson's stands?"

"She looks like a hooker," Trapp said. "She wears too much makeup."

They drove back to the West Side, stopping to talk to a uniformed patrolman, Steve D'Anto. "In four years," D'Anto said, "I've never seen it so quiet. The girls are really scared. I think they've gone to Montreal for the Olympics."

"I'm not working, you bastards," they heard 15 minutes later from one of the contacts, a part-time prostitute named Pat who owned a small boutique in Boston. "You guys are really stupid. This law sucks and there's going to be a lot of trouble if you keep enforcing it. What about the girls on junk? They're going to get the money one way or another. They're going to start mugging and stealing. Is this just for the Convention, you hypocrites? Fuck the Democrats." *

At 10:48, Dorothy Bush began the roll call of states for the Democratic nomination for president of the United States.

* New York's prostitute policy during the Convention was almost an exact duplicate of its official "Rough on Tramps" plan for the 1924 Convention. According to the *New York Times* of June 24, 1924, "The District Attorney gave instructions to all assistants to see that all persons without visible means of support were sent to jail without bail."

"Alabama!"

"Madam Chairman, fellow delegates, Democrats of America," Bob Wilson said, "Alabama delegates are proud to be part of this . . ." Delegates in other states began to shout—"C'mon!" . . . "Vote!"—they thought Wilson was going to make a speech. And he was. Bob Strauss had promised the Alabama delegation three minutes from the floor to praise Wallace—"our wounded warrior," Wilson's text called him—when the chairman thought a sop might foster Convention unity by keeping the Alabaman's name out of nomination. But the Convention was having none of it, booing and yelling as the poor state senator tried to go on. Finally, almost in tears, he quit. Alabama cast 30 votes for Jimmy Carter and 5 votes for George Wallace—Larry Morris and four other delegates held out to the end.

The last five Wallacemen headed for the exit. They were stopped by a reporter from the *New York Times*—Alabama walkouts, after all, were kind of a routine feature of Democratic conventions. Why are you leaving?

"I'm hungry," Morris said.

"Alaska!"

As Alaska gave him its 10 votes, Jimmy Carter walked across the 50-by-20-foot living room of his Americana suite and sat down on a couch with his mother watching three television sets broadcasting the CBS, NBC, and ABC versions of the balloting. At their feet, in pajamas and playing with chopsticks, were the candidate's 8-year-old daughter, Amy, and his 11-month-old grandson, Jason. Four generations of Carters, a family moment—complete with a six-man Pool crew adjusting television lights; Teddy White and Richard Reeves, taking notes for books; Hunter Thompson; Stan Cloud for *Time* magazine; and two wire service correspondents. The room was a stage set; the play, of course, was *The Royal Family*—and when the television camera went on, America saw only winning mother and son, then son stood and scooped up great-grandson, whereupon granddaughter leaped into son's lap and mother said, "She's jealous."

"California!"
California, where Jerry Brown had clobbered Carter in the state's June 8 primary, cast 205 votes for its governor, 73 for Carter, and 2 for Mo Udall. Brown himself watched on television, pacing nervously and grabbing a handful of nuts and raisins from a table in his Hotel McAlpin "suite."

"It is time," Brown said, "for the prisoner of the McAlpin to make his move."

As the Carter total climbed toward the magic number of 1,505, someone changed the "Carter Country—Population 1,505+" sign in front of the Carter trailer compound just outside the main arena, where Ringling Brothers, Barnum & Bailey kept their elephants a month before—and put up a new one that read ". . . Population 230,000,000."

"Massachusetts!"
"Massachusetts passes."
Passes! In the Carter delegate-communication trailer, heads turned toward Joseph Timilty, a Massachusetts state senator, who was one of the candidate's 21 floor leaders—the captain in charge of knowing what was going on in the Massachusetts delegation.

"Massachusetts passes!" he shouted. "Massachusetts passes? You've got to be shitting me. This is a joke. You've got to be shitting me." He obviously did not have the vaguest idea of what was happening. Like almost all the Carter captains, Timilty's appointment was political debt repayment or celebrity recognition like the appointments of a star-studded group that included Senators Birch Bayh and Thomas Eagleton, Theodore Sorensen, and Frank Mankiewicz. The captains were rarely with their ships— they were either being interviewed or just hanging around the trailer, as Timilty unhappily was at the moment.

"Jesus," said Peter Emerson, the press assistant assigned to the Carter trailer camp, "if we ever had a real fight or a second ballot we'd be dead. The well-oiled Carter machine."

"Missouri!"

Missouri cast 58 of its 71 votes for Carter, and Annetta St. Clair, the political science teacher who was having trouble with photographers, waved a sign saying: "Let's Send Amy to Washington." She had made it that morning with the green markers and blank posterboard passed out in the Carter hospitality suite at the Drake Hotel—she went to the suite each morning for a free breakfast of rolls and coffee to save money. Above her in the VVIP section, Rosalynn Carter began waving to her and mouthed the words: can I have your sign? *

Mrs. St. Clair walked into the Carter section past Senators Gary Hart and Hubert Humphrey, who were being kept standing by Mark Gasarch's aides. "Jesus," grumbled Humphrey. "There's got to be a better way."

"New Hampshire!"

"New Hampshire, the first-in-the-nation primary," said Lucille Kelley, "proudly gives 15 votes to Jimmy Carter and 2 for Morris Udall."

It was the proudest moment of her life—she figured she

* The phrase "hospitality suite" appeared in Carter campaign memos after June 10. Before that date, internal memos projected a total of 1,000 to 1,250 Carter delegates and the same rooms were called "hotel command posts."

was just about the first person in the country outside his
family and closest friends to believe in Jimmy Carter—
but she was in great pain. She wore a cervical collar, from
her automobile accident, and a hard hat—a white plastic
construction helmet that someone had given her as a joke.
She left the hall immediately, saying she did not feel well
enough to talk with two men who came up to her and said
they wanted to discuss insurance and to give her a tour
of other delegations to show her that, overnight, the state
delegation standards had been bound more tightly to chairs
with copper wire and actually bolted to the floor in alternate
sections. Within a short time, insurance adjustors representing New York City, Madison Square Garden, and the
Democratic National Committee were suggesting that Miss
Kelley should sue the Iowa delegation—after all, it was
their standard that split her skull.

The count was at 1,026½.

"New Jersey!"

"New Jersey casts all its 108 votes for the next president
of the United States, Jimmy Carter."

"All right, New Jersey. Yeah!" Carter said at the Americana, punching a fist into the air.

"No. No. No! No!" Francis Gorman, normally the
mildest of men, was shouting. He jumped out of his seat,
scuttling to the aisle and began to push toward Dugan,
yelling: "You bum! You made me a liar. I told you I promised my kids I'd vote for Jerry Brown."

Gorman stopped and wheeled around. He wanted to get
out of the building and headed for an exit. Now Dugan
was chasing him. "Fran . . . Fran . . . I wish that hadn't
happened. Of all people, I wouldn't want to do that to you."

"Well, Jim, you did."

Martin Jelin, the man who remembered the 1924 Convention so well, watched Gorman and Dugan and thought

of how he would describe what happened to his family and friends: "This man Dugan didn't play good politics. He dealt with the delegation dishonestly. He wants to be governor, but I think this will hurt him. There were eight delegates sticking with Brown and Humphrey, and Dugan said to them, to each one he said, 'Look, I have 107 other delegates here for Carter and only you standing between us and a unanimous delegation.' Ha! Now they knew about Dugan. He listened to no one."

"Ohio!"

This was going to be it, and the noise level in the Garden was building. At 11:11, Christine Gitlin, a serious harpsichordist from Berea who had been attracted to Carter two years before because he had talked with her about music instead of politics, said: "Madam Chairman, as chairperson of the Ohio delegation, of this nation's largest delegation pledged to Jimmy Carter, I am proud and honored . . . to cast in the spirit of unity, love, and victory in November, *132 votes for Jimmy Carter.*"

Bob Strauss pointed up to Peter Duchin's orchestra and they hit "Happy Days are Here Again"—Franklin Roosevelt's song. Mazie Woodruff jumped up in the North Carolina delegation, jiggling a sign that said: "Peanut Butter Is Love. Spread Some Around Today." Lillian Carter reached up and placed the palm of her right hand against her son's cheek. "It's been a long time," he said. "I'm glad it's Ohio"—he had managed to convince the press that it was *the* important primary on June 8, so that his victory over Udall there was interpreted as somehow more significant than Brown's California triumph or Jim Dugan's mastery of New Jersey. Jody Powell, Carter's Tonto, the man who had scheduled the Philadelphia press conference that no one came to, walked up to his Lone Ranger— Powell was wearing one black shoe and a sneaker because of a sprained ankle—stuck out his hand, and said: "Congratulations."

And Joe Kaselak, who had slipped into the Ohio delegation, stood behind Chris Gitlin, raising his arms and cheering. He wore the credentials of Milton Tenenbaum, a Udall delegate who had gone back to the Sheraton rather than watch his man come in second for the last time.

The vote when the roll call was completed was: Carter—2,238½; Udall—329½; Brown—300½; Wallace—57; McCormack—22; Church—19; Jackson—10; Humphrey—10; Harris—9; Milton Shapp—2; Robert Byrd—1; Cesar Chavez—1; Leon Jaworski—1; Barbara Jordan—1; Edward Kennedy—1; Jennings Randolph—1; Fred Stover—1; and 3½ abstentions.

The California delegation microphone was switched on for Jerry Brown's moment at 11:34—one of the reasons Strauss wanted Brown on the floor was that the chairman also could have switched that mike off if he didn't like what the young governor was saying. Brown made it brief, calling for unity, for victory, and then switching "California's 278 votes" to Carter. What about the other 2? California had 280 votes. "They're floating in the hall someplace," he said.

"Big deal, Jerry!" someone shouted in the Carter command trailer. "Jerry's Born Again," came the answer from across the crowd, laughing and raising beer cans in celebration. Rick Hutcheson, Carter's deputy campaign manager and chief delegate counter, had ordered that no beer be allowed inside the trailer—the order was in force for about a half-hour until Hamilton Jordan, Hutcheson's boss, came in and said, "Where's the beer? I want a beer."

While Brown did his thing, Dan Courtenay's phone rang four levels below. The NYPD commander picked it up and heard Cliff Cassidy, the DNC's security chief: "The Brown

motorcade will not be allowed back up the VIP ramp."
Courtenay relayed the message, telling his cops not to let
Brown's car inside the Garden. "A parting shot," Courtenay
said. "He held out on them, so they make him walk out
and try to find his car."

The permanent chairman of the Convention, Representative Lindy Boggs of Louisiana, following ritual more than
100 years old, announced: "The chair will now appoint a
committee to inquire if he will accept the nomination."

"That's two decisions I have to make before tomorrow,"
said Jimmy Carter at the Americana, where his vice-presidential choice was to be announced at ten o'clock in the
morning. "Goodnight, Mr. President," said his mother,
getting up from the couch.

Inside the Carter trailer camp, Hamilton Jordan bounded
through the crowd of his workers, hugging Pat Caddell,
who was smoking a cigar about two sizes too big for him.
"Yeeeow!" Jordan yelled, leaping to the top of the stairs of
one of the trailers. "Now that we're through the primaries . . ." he began, and the group suddenly quieted. He
laughed: "I'd like to announce that we are firing all the
women and blacks!

"Y'all did great! Great!" he yelled. Then he quieted
down and said: "It's hard to grasp what's happening." He
stopped. "I don't think any of us understands it completely,
what's happening . . ." He stopped again. "Not bad for a
bunch of dumb southerners!"

By midnight, the trailers were locked up with telephones
ringing unanswered inside. Standing by them, Peter Emerson, the young Carter press aide who arranged television
interviews for Jordan and Caddell and the others, said: "I
didn't get interviewed again tonight. They promised me

I'd get interviewed." It was hard to tell whether he was kidding or not. "I've only got one more night."

The Carter trailer party, Hamilton Jordan presiding with sporadic rebel yells, moved uptown to the 21st floor of the Americana. Inside the nominee's suite, the Carters and the staff just kind of milled around, hugging and kissing each other. There was nothing to drink and Rosalynn Carter apologized for that a couple of times before saying, "Wait!" She went behind the unused bar and came back holding a box of Georgia peaches.

Jordan made a little speech, thanking everyone in sight, but singling out one man: "Bob Lipshutz. No one made more of a contribution to the campaign and received less credit than Bob Lipshutz."

Robert Lipshutz, a 54-year-old Atlanta lawyer and a leader of the city's Jewish community, was the treasurer of the Carter campaign and, in many ways, the overall strategy of the campaign had been dictated by the financial strategy. In the simplest terms, the strategy was to show well in the Iowa precinct caucuses on January 19, to stimulate press interest in Carter, and then spend as much money as could be raised and borrowed—from friendly Atlanta banks and Georgia business interests—to win the New Hampshire and Florida primaries. Despite innumerable reports of Carter master plans and organizational genius, there was no plan and precious little organization after the Florida vote on March 9. The Carters gambled that their early victories would generate fundraising, organizational, and press "momentum"—the political cliché used to describe what is happening when no one is sure.

"New Hampshire looks good," said a mailgram Carter sent out on February 10. "Victory in Florida can seal nomination. To win there we must reach people who don't attend rallies. Paid television is key. Must postpone $100,-

000 planned for TV scheduled for week of February 23 unless have funds. Can you raise and send $5,000." *

Cash flow all that time was maintained from Atlanta. In May, the Carter campaign debt was $1.84 million against anticipated matching fund receipts of only $800,000 from the Federal Election Commission. The difference was made up primarily by Fulton National Bank ($601,584), Citizens and Southern Bank ($175,000), and Rafshoon Advertising ($302,210). Carter was campaigning against "special interests" while being underwritten by mostly unsecured loans from banks especially interested in the future of southern business and by Jerry Rafshoon, who was both aware and open concerning the impact of his Carter connection on his agency's prospects. "Why should I go to Washington with Jimmy?" he said. "If he's president, I'm going to make a fortune in Atlanta. People are already coming around who never knew I existed before." The same was true of Pat Caddell—his polling firm, Cambridge Opinion Research, had just picked up the government of Saudi Arabia as a client providing 10 percent of the firm's total revenues—and of Charlie Kirbo's courtship by corporate America.

"There's just one thing I'd like to say," Carter said after Hamilton Jordan's little speech. "I'd hate to run against this crowd." At 1:50, Carter came out of the suite into the cor-

---

* The Carter campaign, which spent $658,837 in 1975 and $2,086,591 in the first three months of 1976, depended heavily on regional fundraising parties and events, including rock music concerts organized by Phil Walden of Macon, Georgia, the president of Capricorn Records, whose biggest act, the Allman Brothers, raised $350,000. Smaller events were set up by the recipients of mailgrams, who were restricted to personal contributions of $1,000 under Federal election laws. The Carter mailing lists were compiled from his Georgia campaign lists, people he met while traveling for the DNC Congressional Committee in 1974, and contacts he made personally acting as the host to each convention which came to Atlanta during his term as governor—Atlanta is the fourth largest convention city in the country.

ridors where more junior members of the staff were celebrating. He waved a copy of the *New York Daily News*—IT'S CARTER covered half the front page—and said it again: "How about that? I'd hate to run against this crowd. Thank you all."

At 2:00 A.M., Barry Jagoda, Carter television adviser, decided to leave the candidate's floor and go down to a staff party in Albert Hall. Stepping into the elevator on the 20th floor of the Americana, he saw a small man in his 30s wearing a bouquet of important-looking plastic and paper around his neck and carrying sheaves of papers. "I know you, don't I?" Jagoda said.

The man didn't answer. "I'm Barry Jagoda, don't we know each other? Aren't you famous?"

The man whirled, shouting: "I'll pay you the goddamn $200. You know I'm good for it."

"Marty Evans! You no-good son-of-a-bitch. I should kill you!" Jagoda inspected plastic and paper. The most impressive piece was one dated 1969, stating that Evans was an "Authorized Representative—New York City Department of Social Services." "What are you doing here? You cheated me out of $200. How did you get in here?"

"Don't shout, Barry. I'm putting together a cable television network, and I'm meeting with the Carter people . . ."

"You're what? You crook! I *am* 'the Carter people' . . ." Jagoda lapsed into spasms of laughter and swearing. Evans began showing strangers Xeroxed clippings about himself. One from the *Village Voice* called him "The Worst Man in New York"—among other things, Evans had seduced a series of young women by claiming that he was Jack Newfield, a *Voice* writer. Most of the stories dealt with his acquittal on rape charges brought by a Wellesley College student who testified that he lured her to an apartment after

Joe Kaselak made the networks.

Ann Compton woke up with canker sores.

They chained down the TV in the Railroad Lounge.

Barry Jagoda angrily warned the Carter campaign it was headed for its own Watergate.

Jim Gammill was sure his phone was being tapped by CBS. ▶

Mazie Woodruff wouldn't sit in the balcony.

Edward Bennett Williams had never been so humiliated;
Charles Kirbo had never been so much in demand.

Fritz Efaw was intimidated by Bella Abzug's enforcers.

Mo Udall ignored Sarah Kovner's tears.

Mimi Gurbst took Preston Robert Tisch along to carry the tickets.

Rick Neustadt fed Walter Cronkite his lines.

Rocky Pomerance and Dan Courtenay handled the final humiliation of Jerry Brown.

◀ Clare Smith tried to find Hunter Thompson; Mary Ault ▶ would have liked to, but had to spend her evenings with the creeps.

Robert Strauss cued **Abe Beame,**
applauded **Averill Harriman,**
took care of **Mrs. Strauss,**
and came to terms with **Pat Caddell** and **Jerry Rafshoon.**
He was always smiling—except when he wasn't.

Norm Leonard turned on the lights—
sometimes.

Sal Lividini worried about hookers.

Jim Gallagher kept the Minnesotas off the streets.

Mark Gasarch knew that
Phyllis Wagner knew that *he* knew.

Dick Celeste made an impression, sort of.

Walter Mondale listened to Robert Strauss, who was on his knees.

John Glenn could look forward to mowing the lawn.

Lucille Kelley came back in a helmet.

Joan Mondale cared about Day Care—
but Rosalynn Carter cared more.

Bill vanden Heuvel hoped that Hamilton had been watching.

identifying himself as a psychologist researching the lives of young women.*

Jagoda pointed Evans out to the security guards at the door of Albert Hall: "Don't let that man in. He's the worst con artist in the country." Five minutes later, Evans was inside, introducing himself to Jody Powell and saying: "I've been working with your people, Barry Jagoda and others, on setting up a cable TV network for the campaign and . . ."

Annie went to work at the corner of Broadway and 43rd Street after the Convention session ended. Three times within the hour after midnight, she was approached by men wearing Convention credentials or "Carter" buttons. Each time, a policeman stepped from around the corner— each time it was a different cop—and said something like: "Don't pick her up. She'll rob you."

That happened to be true in Annie's case, but when the usual run of Times Square business came her way, there were no cops. She made $175 for the night.

Part of the NYPD's Convention plan was to station uniformed patrolmen on corners where they usually would not be, places they did not want delegates to wander into by mistake. The Bottomless Pit or Chez Paree, fine—you pay your money, you take your choice—or homosexual "singles" bars downtown like the Ramrod or Peter Rabbit. But not the Toilet. There was a cop on West 14th Street near the Hudson River—Jim Gallagher of the Morals Squad was worried that a gay delegate or reporter was going to ask where the action was and be told about the Toilet on the fourth floor of the loft building at 400 West 14th Street. Maybe Omaha wasn't ready for a place where the sign over the checkroom said, "Coats—50¢. Clothes—

* Evans was convicted of trespassing—the apartment was not his—and of escaping from police in the incident.

$1.00"—and the seats were old toilets and there was a stage, bare except for a mattress, for amateur entertainers. Separated from the main barroom by a plywood wall was "the church" with its "confessionals"—thin plywood dividers with a line of holes cut at various heights and kneeling pads on either side. One side of each divider wall was marked "Donor" and the other "Receiver." Completely anonymous—the Donors offered golden showers, fist fucks, the works.

Things were tough all over. The night boss at the Uptown Mansion on East 62nd Street, three doors off Park Avenue, was watching television with six of her girls. She sipped chablis—pronouncing it to rhyme with "miss"— from a plastic glass and said the Convention was a disaster for business, even though some other houses, like the Townhouse of East 38th Street, were staying open until 4:00 A.M. instead of their usual 2:00 A.M. "Politicians are afraid these days," she said, pointing to the blank spaces on the printed schedule that controlled traffic in the house's eight bedrooms. "The newspapers. That creep Wayne Hays . . .

"I don't like Jimmy Carter at all. He doesn't understand us. He doesn't understand cities. New York is falling apart and they give us someone from Georgia? What does he know about us? It's not safe to go out anymore around here, and this is one of the best neighborhoods in the city. Nobody cares about law and order, about right and wrong. It's a disgrace."

Mark Gasarch decided to do his postsession drinking at P. J. Clarke's at the corner of Third Avenue and 54th Street, one of the city's most popular late-night stops. They were four-deep at the bar; he could hardly get in the door. Someone looked at his credential and said, "Security!" A path to the bar opened—"I guess they thought Jimmy Carter was behind me and wanted a hamburger."

He saw Donald Carey, an aide-supervisor and the son of New York's Governor Hugh Carey, and sat down to tell him about Phyllis Cerf Wagner. "I'll make you a bet," said Carey, "if she has to make 50 phone calls, she'll be on that list tomorrow."

The next day's *New York Post* reported Jimmy Carter's nomination in a long story that ended: "The Rev. Robert N. Deming of Kansas City, Mo., delivered the closing prayer."

But he didn't. Father Deming was neither seen nor heard from after he escaped from Robert Strauss's office behind the podium. The benediction was actually given by the Reverend Leo J. Daley of Xavier High School, the priest who happened to pick up the phone when Congressman Drinan called during the middle of the session.

☒ # Thursday

July 15

W alter Mondale was sitting in the living room of the Kennedy Suite on the 34th floor of the Carlyle Hotel, the suite John F. Kennedy had often used while president. At the Carlyle, the bellmen wore white gloves, but Mondale was wearing old slacks and sneakers, alternately pacing to the windows and drinking coffee, then trying to make conversation with his wife, Joan, and three staff members. No one could think of much to say. The telephone rang—Mondale's administrative assistant, Richard Moe, looked at his watch—at 8:26 A.M.

"Senator Mondale? Governor Carter would like to speak with you," said Greg Schneiders.

"Hi, did I wake you up?" Carter said. "Would you like to run with me?" Mondale threw his right thumb up.

"I would be deeply honored," Mondale said. He turned around and hugged his wife.

Carter asked Mondale not to tell anyone—"not a soul" —of the call and told the Minnesota senator to leave for the Americana when his press conference began there at 10:00. The Secret Service arrived at 9:30, and Mrs. Mondale called her three children at home in Washington. "Turn on the television at ten o'clock," she told them. Is it daddy? "Just turn on the television and watch."

Schneiders placed the call to John Glenn at 8:40. There was no answer. "Operator," Carter's assistant said to the woman on the switchboard at the Sheraton, "is there another number where we can reach Senator Glenn?"

"We're not allowed to give out that information," she said.

"This is a very important call from Governor Jimmy Carter," Schneiders said, and the operator said she would try the other number but would not give it out. "It's busy," she told Schneiders.

"Can you break in on that call?" Schneiders said. "This is an *urgent* call from *Jimmy Carter*. I'm sure Senator Glenn would like to talk to him."

"I'm sorry, sir, hotel policy . . ."

"Would you send someone to that room and tell Senator Glenn that Jimmy Carter is trying to reach him?"

"I'm sorry, sir, hotel policy . . ."

Schneiders hung up and Carter said, "If you can't get him in five minutes, I want you to take a taxi over there and tell him to call me."

Exactly five minutes later, Schneiders got through. As Glenn answered, at 8:51, Schneiders said Carter would be on in a moment and then came back to say, could Glenn please hold on, President Ford was on another line. The president wanted to congratulate Carter on his nomination.

Glenn waited. After three minutes, Carter came on and said, "John, I've called to let you know that I've picked someone else. I enjoyed meeting you, John, and I want you to be my lifelong friend. I'd also like to count on your help in the campaign."

"I'll do whatever I can," Glenn said. He shrugged and turned to his wife, Annie, and said: "Well, we wondered who was going to cut the grass at home this weekend. It's going to be me."

The secret—Mondale's name—held, which was a rare thing in politics. The reason was that no one except Jimmy Carter knew for sure until he told his wife two minutes before the first phone call, then walked out of their bedroom and told Schneiders, "Call Mondale." The only other people in the living room were Marie Hartnett, Schneiders' fiancée, Charles Zeboril, the head of Carter's Secret Service detail; and Stanley Tretick, the campaign photographer. "Oh, God," Tretick said, "I'm not leaving this room until ten o'clock—if this leaks, I don't want to be blamed."

Zane Tankel, the president of Collier Lithography, called Jerry Rafshoon, Carter's media man, just after 9:00 A.M. and said, "Give me a hint. I'm holding the pressroom, but it would save us a lot of money if we had a clue." Tankel was still holding the button and poster order featuring Jimmy Carter and his vice-presidential nominee. Tankel had gotten the business by going to Atlanta in December, 1975, and asking for it—as he had asked a dozen other potential Democratic candidates. "When you go national . . ." he had said then, thinking to himself: Shit, these people are never going national! Rafshoon told him to turn on his television like everyone else.

"I have . . ." Carter said at the press conference, hesitating, "I have two announcements to make. One is that I've decided to accept the nomination of president. And the other one is that I've asked to serve as my running mate—if the delegates will approve—Senator Walter Mondale from Minnesota."

"Mondale. Go!" Zane Tankel shouted into the desk intercom that connected with his pressroom.

Mondale, followed by live network cameras, arrived at the Americana press conference 20 minutes later, beginning: "I heard the first part of your news conference in which you remarked that I was up at 6:30; actually, I was up much earlier than that, trying to fix my phone, which hadn't rung for three days."

"You son-of-a-bitch!" Tom Hayden shouted at his television set. Not Tom Hayden, the California politician, but "the real Tom Hayden," as he was known at Madison Square Garden—Thomas J. Hayden, division manager of New York Telephone Company, the man in overall charge of 500 New York Tel people who had worked seven months to plan and build the Convention phone system: 7,000 units, 13,700 miles of wire, 77 video lines for television transmission, and complaints about the cost of almost every single unit. The vice-presidential phones, of course, were $229.49 each, and the *Washington Star* paid $3,174 for six lines and an intercom before a call was made. Besides all that, his men were being attacked by elephants. While New York Tel's finest were preparing their main workroom in May, holes were smashed in the walls around them by two fighting elephants of the Garden's spring tenant, the Ringling Brothers, Barnum & Bailey Circus. "If Sabu had given the wrong order in Swahili," said Hayden, "we all would have had it." *

Now this bum, Mondale, was on national television say-

* The telephone that would have been the most expensive at the Convention—a $12,000 Picturephone—was considered by the Carter campaign but finally rejected when the candidate decided the price was just too high. The phone, with small television screens allowing the parties at either end to see each other, would have been a special line from Jimmy Carter's Americana suite to his delegate-communication trailer at Madison Square Garden, allowing the candidate to show and tell to wavering delegates and VIPs. The high cost of telephone service was the result of a "Special Convention Charge"—often amounting to three or four times the cost of the service itself—added to all Convention telephone bills, including the charges to networks for video lines, because of the regulations of the Federal Election Commission and New York Telephone's interpretation of rulings by the New York State Public Service Com-

ing that his phone was broken. Hayden, who had joined New York Tel at 18 as an apprentice repairman, knew what would happen next. Vice-presidents would begin calling and holding meetings: Bad publicity! Bad publicity! It looked bad for Ma Bell, Tom. Besides, the real Tom Hayden was a Republican.

The Mondales' three children—Teddy, 18, Eleanor, 16, and William, 14—were already on their way to Washington's National Airport to catch the Eastern Airlines shuttle to New York. Their mother had called them again right after Carter's announcement and told them to take the train, the Metroliner, to New York to save a few dollars and avoid the television cameras at the airports. Television? The three Mondale children voted unanimously to take a plane.

After their husbands' joint press conference, Rosalynn Carter and Joan Mondale, who had met each other only once before, went up to the 21st floor to talk. Mrs. Mondale said that she did not believe that her children would take to campaigning, and Mrs. Carter, who, with her children, had done things like going around restaurants shaking hands rather than waste the time between ordering and eat-

---

mission. The FEC ruled that any financial losses absorbed by the company during the Convention would constitute illegal campaign contributions to the Democrats. The PSC rulings were interpreted to mean that New York Tel could not pass along Convention costs to its regular subscribers—in the past, the people who lived in Convention cities unknowingly underwrote the events. So New York Tell billed at its actual calculated cost and demanded large cash deposits—$90,000 from the Carter campaign alone. Part of New York Tel's attitude had to do with the fact that the Democratic National Committee still owed various Bell System companies $1,038,000 from its 1968 Convention and the debt-ridden campaigns of Hubert Humphrey and Robert Kennedy the same year.

ing, said, "I found out one thing and you will, too. You can do anything you have to do." *

Later, the two wives went downstairs for their own press conference. Mrs. Mondale was asked what sort of activities she would be involved in if her husband was vice-president. "Day care centers," she said, adding that her husband had introduced a bill . . .

Mrs. Carter stepped to the microphone before Mrs. Mondale could finish, saying softly: "I've become very concerned about day care centers . . . I'm sure Mrs. Mondale would be capable of helping me with anything I try to do."

As the press conference was breaking up, Mrs. Carter mentioned that a supporter had sent Frisbees to her family. Photographers immediately began to clamor for shots of the wives and Amy Carter throwing the discs—which they obligingly did again and again. Thus did Irv Lander of the World Frisbee Association, Inc., who had called volunteer Alan Fein on Tuesday afternoon, get his products plugged on television and in the newspapers—which is why he sent them over in the first place.

Pat Sweeney's date in Criminal Court was at 9:30 in the morning. He had gotten his Monte Carlo, broken window and all, back from the car pound the day before when the Ohio company he leased it from sent a telecopy of the registration to the New York police.

As he walked into Judge J. J. O'Hara's courtroom, Sweeney was approached by a young woman holding two

---

* One of the negatives in the consideration of John Glenn for vice-president, according to Carter staff members, was that his wife, Annie, stutters, and Mrs. Carter did not believe that she would be an effective campaigner.

small children. "My husband didn't do this," she said. "You got the wrong person."

"Are you crazy, lady?" Sweeney almost shouted. "I caught him in my car!" She began to cry, "Please, drop the charges." He walked away.

Then a man walked up to Sweeney, saying he was the Legal Aid attorney assigned to defend Roy Kisowski and asked him to drop the charges. Sweeney said he was not going to agree to anything.

"This isn't Ohio. We'll get postponements every week, and you'll be back here every week. Sooner or later, you'll get tired of coming and the charges will be dropped."

"I thought your duty was to make sure justice is served."

"My duty is to get him off."

John O'Donnell, the assistant prosecutor assigned to the case, was the next one to talk to Sweeney, advising him to agree to lesser charges—"A trial will be a pain to everyone."

"I want a trial. The man broke into my car."

O'Donnell took Sweeney to see Judge O'Hara in his chambers. The judge told him that it was very rare for people to go to jail for such "minor" crimes in New York, that O'Donnell and the Legal Aid attorney were telling him the truth. Sweeney gave in.

Kisowski, who had a record of more than a dozen arrests, was put on probation for a year and ordered to pay Sweeney $100 for the smashed window. The defendant left the courthouse, but Sweeney had to go to the Police Property Clerk's office to fill out the forms to reclaim his camera. It was 4:30 before he was finished and headed for the Garden to hear Jimmy Carter's acceptance speech.

"You know," said Patrolman Ryan, who had arrested Kisowski, "there's no way you're going to get that $100."

In mid-afternoon, Senator Mondale sent the draft of the acceptance speech he had been working on for three days— a contingency—over to Carter's speechwriter, Pat Anderson. Generally approving, Anderson suggested that Mondale look over sections which had been dropped from Carter's speech. The senator said he liked a couple of them, especially one line: "We have just lived through the greatest political scandal in American history and are now led by a president who pardoned the person who did it."

Arthur V. N. Brooks, a wealthy Cleveland lawyer and Ohio state representative, had been elected a Udall delegate from the state's 22nd Congressional District, a liberal, heavily Jewish suburban district. Because of the number of Jewish voters, Joe Kaselak had run there as an alternate delegate pledged to Senator Henry Jackson, figuring that the Senator's fervent pro-Israel record would carry him to New York as a legitimate part of the Convention. But by the June 8 primary, Jackson had withdrawn as a presidential candidate and Kaselak ran dead last.

Brooks had a ticket on a 6:35 P.M. Amtrak train to Wilmington, Delaware, where he was meeting his family to begin a vacation. He went to the Garden for the afternoon session because he was interested in the final rules debates, then decided "the orgy of togetherness," as he called it, was over for him.

Walking out, Brooks handed his credentials to another Udall delegate. It was Milt Tenenbaum, Kaselak's friend, and he found Joe: "Need anything, buddy?"

Kaselak spent seven hours on the floor—all of it standing up. He made a point of never sitting in a chair—it might be someone else's and there might be a hassle, the kind that attracts ushers and guards and gets gate crashers thrown out. He was on television four times, swearing to himself that this was his Last Hurrah. "Jesus, I've got arthritis already and my legs aren't getting any stronger. It's not easy to go begging every day. But you know, all night people kept coming up to me and saying, 'Joe, I saw you on TV— you looked great!'"

Arthur Brooks was one of the few delegates who was really interested in being at the final afternoon session. The only thing on the agenda was: "Report on Rules—Part II." It was a time for delegates to give their credentials to alternates, or to friends who wanted to sit on the floor even if nothing was happening.

But something was happening. "Rules—Part II" was where Chairman Strauss intended to make his system of controlling Democratic conventions as permanent as anything can be in American politics. And like any good Texas Friday-night poker player, he was using his own cards. His ace in the hole was that, under current rules, all procedural votes referred back to a single sentence in the "Rules Report" section on credentials: "A majority of the Convention eligible to vote shall constitute acceptance of any such motion."

What that meant was that 1,505 votes—a majority of all delegates—would be needed to carry any of the minority reports being considered. A dull afternoon session late in the Convention was the best way to keep delegates away. And many stayed away—packing, shopping, catching up on sleep—making it as difficult as possible to get enough votes to pass minority reports that would destroy the Strauss system. The chairman's plan worked—barely.

Minority Reports Number 4 and Number 6 were the dangerous ones. Number 4 would have amended the rules to require that two-thirds of the delegates to the party's 1978 Mid-Term Conference be elected locally—instead of leaving delegate selection procedures, and control, with the

Democratic National Committee. Number 6 would have reduced the percentage of committee members necessary to bring minority reports before the 1980 convention from Strauss's beloved 25 percent to only 15 percent.

"You can't live with these changes," Strauss told Carter. "The liberals and the weirdos will use them to eat you alive. They'll use the Mid-Term Conference to attack your administration and you'll be at their mercy at the next Convention." The candidate agreed, pledging the support of his delegate-communication trailer operation and his floor captains to fight the minority reports. The only problem was that the Carter trailer-floor system was more impressive as a prop for touring television correspondents than it was for lining up delegate votes. Peter Emerson, the Carter aide who conducted the television tours, said: "We're not sure we can do it, so we won't push too hard. We're afraid to try and publicly fail. Luckily, there's no real organized opposition—we don't think."

Even without opposition, the Carters lost the vote on Number 4, the Mid-Term Conference, by 1,240 to 1,128. The chair then ruled that the required 1,505 votes had not been reached. The motion failed—DNC control was saved by the delegates who weren't there.

The Carter troops were a little more alert on Minority Report Number 6, the 25 percent rule change.

"Look, this is what ruined us in 1972," Frank Mankiewicz told a group of Texas delegates. "If this goes through, the 1980 Convention will be like that. The television networks will set our agenda. They'll focus on the bizarre stuff —homosexual rights, right-to-life."

"Minority reports were important when the National Committees were packed in the old days," he told a California liberal, "now they're representative of the party. There's dissent at every level of the party."

The 15 percent amendment was defeated by a vote of

1,364½ to 1,249. It was close, but Bob Strauss had done the job he hired out to do. "I'll always be grateful to you," Jimmy Carter said. "My people were lost at the end."

The VVIP list, which was expanded to 140 names for the final night, was scheduled to get to Mark Gasarch, the aide-chief, at 4:00 P.M. But Phyllis Cerf Wagner arrived an hour before that, smiling graciously at Gasarch and calling him a fine young man. He knew then that when the list arrived, her name would be on it—Donald Carey had been right.

He immediately seated her in her favored spot in the third row, smiling and bowing as he did it. Then he walked to the back of Section 58, watching her constantly—40 minutes went by before she opened her pocketbook and began fumbling around inside. A cigarette! Gasarch raced down the stairs. "Allow me," he said, reaching for the book of matches in the left-hand pocket of his blue aide blazer— the matches Rick Strauss had given him earlier, her monogrammed matches with a large *C,* for Cerf. He saw her smile—this was going to be his final act of supplication for calling her Mrs. Cerf. But the smile stopped when she saw the matches. Their little game was over.

"I knew. She knew. I knew she knew. She knew I knew."

Dick Celeste had begun to take notes for a newspaper column he was going to do on the Convention. A week before leaving Ohio, his aide, Jerry Austin, had telephoned 100 weekly newspapers in the state, asking them if they would publish an "analysis" by Celeste. Sixty of them said "yes" and the lieutenant governor wrote: "It was a time to bring people back together, a time for building up, perhaps even a time of love."

About his own building up, Celeste said: "I want to

come back here in 1980, and if I come back as governor of Ohio, I want a staff that knows what to do. I don't want them standing around staring at Warren Beatty."

The nominations for vice-president began 15 minutes after the last session of the Convention was called to order at 6:45. There were four: Walter Mondale, and three put up to get some television attention—Fritz Efaw, Ron Dellums, and Gary Benoit, a 22-year-old Massachusetts delegate used for getting Boston antibusing arguments onto prime time.

Robert McGrail spoke first, mentioning Benoit in passing and then talking of "black and white children glaring hate at each other because of a forced situation"—court-ordered busing to racially balance Boston's schools. Very few delegates were paying attention, but Mazie Woodruff was—and getting madder and madder.

The second speaker for Benoit was Boston Councilman Albert ("Dapper") O'Neil. He was into his fourth sentence when Mrs. Woodruff jumped up and grabbed the red phone connecting the North Carolina delegation to the podium. "I want equal time," she shouted. "If they're going to keep this junk up, I want equal time to defend my people. Busing isn't the issue here."

Hugh Cannon, the Convention parliamentarian and a North Carolinian who knew her, happened to answer the podium phone and said: "We've already got one of them off, Mrs. Woodruff. And we're about to kick this one off right now."

Louise Ransom, the Gold Star mother, gave the formal nominating speech for Fritz Efaw, the draft exile—"draft dodger," said Walter Cronkite in introducing the speech on CBS—concluding, to heavy applause: "We cannot bring the dead back to life, but we can make amends to the living.

Total amnesty would be a fitting memorial to the sacrifice of my son."

The delegates could see Convention aides straining to lift Ron Kovic, in his wheelchair, up to the podium. The Garden became quiet, quieter than it had been for Barbara Jordan.

"Guilt!" said Don Katz, a writer who helped organize the Efaw nomination. "In a world of Jimmy Carter abstractions, where the operative nouns were words like 'love' and 'trust,' we were thinking of rubbing the most real of dirty wars in their faces. Mike Ransom, Louise's son, was killed on Mother's Day. Ron Kovic was born on the Fourth of July. It would be a cavalcade of Vietnam memories. Was Bicentennial America ready to have its nose rubbed in the shit of Vietnam—even for 15 minutes?" *

Kovic, unlike Efaw, was neither shy nor reluctant about his moment in the eye of the cameras. He gloried in it, exultantly calling his father on Long Island that afternoon to say: "Dad, I'm going to be on TV tonight. I'm going to nominate a friend of mine to be vice-president of the United States."

Before being lifted up, Kovic had been arguing with Don Katz, who was using a felt-tip pen to slash long sections of his speech out of the text. "You can't take those lines out," Kovic shouted. "I ache for each one of those lines."

"I know, I know," said Katz, "but you can't get down on the Kennedys in front of these people. And you can't let them crawl under their chairs. You have to let them be able to look at you." Besides, Katz said, Don Webster, the CBS correspondent covering Efaw, had told them that the network would carry the speech only if it was cut to about two minutes.

* Don Katz's words are from his account of the Efaw nomination published August 26, 1976, in *Rolling Stone.*

On stage, Kovic thrust his arms into the air and the crowd applauded. He did it again and they cheered, they stood. It was the same reception that they had given Hubert Humphrey—who once called Vietnam "our great adventure"—when he nominated Mondale 20 minutes before. And Kovic drew the same energy from it that Humphrey had.

"I am the living dead. Your Memorial Day on wheels. Your Yankee Doodle Dandy. Your John Wayne come home. Your Fourth of July firecracker, exploding in the grave. . . . I wanted to be a good American. I cried when I saw men burning their draft cards. I was angry. I shot and killed a man. When he was pulled in, I suddenly realized I had accidentally killed one of my own men. . . . And, tonight, I have the proud distinction of nominating Fritz Efaw for vice-president of the United States. Welcome home, Fritz."

Efaw, seconding his own nomination, could not match that power, but he carefully laid out his case for amnesty for both draft resisters and deserters, ending: "I am proud to come to this Convention to represent war resisters. . . . I respectfully decline this nomination for vice-president of the United States. I seek no office and no further recognition." *

As Efaw had begun to speak, Morris Udall got up to leave the floor with an entourage of assistants. Sarah Kovner, the New York Udall delegate who had helped organize the Efaw nomination, saw him and pushed toward him: "Mo! Mo, stop. You should be listening to this."

* Efaw returned to Oklahoma on July 24, spending 36 hours in a county jail in the period before Federal Judge Fred Daugherty dismissed all charges against him August 12, on the grounds that the Stillwell, Oklahoma, draft board had not kept him properly informed of the status of his 1969 appeal to be excused from military service as a conscientious objector.

Udall did not turn. Ms. Kovner, who had been crying since Kovic began speaking, screamed: "Mo! Mo, I'm sorry I voted for you!"

At 7:30, Macy Jones and Charles Reisler, two account executives for New York advertising agencies, came up to the Democratic National Committee's offices on the second floor of the Statler Hilton. They asked for credentials under the name of Jones. The receptionist opened a desk drawer and began flipping through envelopes. The one on top said: "Fitzgerald—Michigan." She looked up and said, "I'm sorry, we don't seem to have any Jones."

"Oh," said Reisler, "then it must be under Fitzgerald."

"Yes, here it is." There were two "Honored Guest" passes in the envelope.

"I suppose Mondale is okay," Clare Smith wrote in her diary. "I don't know much about him. I trust Jimmy's judgment." She tried to pay attention to the speeches but, as usual, it was hard to hear on the floor—"What a mess. Reporters and garbage everywhere." Besides, it was cold, even though Rick Weber had given her his suit jacket to wear over her long-sleeved dress and sweater. He sat beside her and said he couldn't keep their date that night. Something very important had come up. Could they have breakfast instead? Sure, Clare said.

Fritz Mondale was okay with almost everybody. The vice-presidential roll call ended with 2,817 votes for the Minnesotan, 20 for Representative Dellums, 12 for Gary Benoit, 11 for Fritz Efaw, and 148 for persons known and unknown, including Hunter Thompson.

The most exciting moment in the roll call, though, had

nothing to do with candidates. When Dorothy Bush called, "Texas!" the state's delegates jumped up with a card display that read: TEXAS LOVES NEW YORK CITY!

It was a fix. Bob Strauss immediately popped to the microphone with Mayor Abraham Beame and the Texans began to sing, "We love you, New York." Beame responded, "Thank you, Texans; thank you, everyone."

But Strauss had not set up the scene that night when the Kelley family of Rogers, Arkansas, in the Ozark Mountains, had dinner at La Toque Blanche at First Avenue and 50th Street. Eugene Kelley, a lawyer and farmer in the town of 13,000, was one of the delegates who brought his family with him—or part of it, his wife and the two oldest of their five children. After dinner, his 15-year-old daughter, Jodie, said: "Let's not go back with the delegation tomorrow. Let's stay another five or six days."

The real Tom Hayden, New York Telephone's Convention Manager, started to walk onto the floor at 10:30 wearing his "Operations" credential. He was stopped by a Secret Service agent: "I'm sorry, sir, I can't honor your pass. The floor is being secured for Governor Carter's entrance."

The security was the tightest of the Convention and the small lights in the security Skybox high above the podium was showing a "Blue" bomb condition, signalling those who knew where to look that a search was under way. Hayden wandered through the corridors behind the podium and sat down outside the DNC's Garden offices. Senator Hubert Humphrey walked out the door past him, and Hayden said hello, thinking that if he was not secure enough to be on the floor, how come he was back here with Hubert Humphrey? Then Senator Edmund Muskie came out. Then Lillian Carter. Then Rosalynn Carter holding hands with her daughter, Amy, who was asking Mickey DeHart, a

Convention aide, to take care of her coloring book. "Good luck, Mrs. Carter," he said, and she smiled.*

Jimmy Carter had arrived in Madison Square Garden at 9:05 P.M., having made the 20-block trip from the Americana in three minutes as 10 NYPD cars and scooters cleared the avenue of traffic for his Chrysler limousine. The Chrysler drove up the ramp on 33rd Street to the fifth level of the Garden, and the nominee went into his VIP trailer—the one set up like a large living room, which had been practically unused until now—where he was met by Jerry Rafshoon and a television makeup man. "What about the lights?" Carter asked.

The Carter people, the television networks, and the DNC had been arguing about the lights since noon. Rafshoon and Barry Jagoda wanted the Garden lights dimmed before Carter's entrance, then a single spotlight in the ceiling would come dramatically on, hitting the podium and—Jimmy Carter! CBS, NBC, and ABC, who would be forced to work in the darkened arena and then keep their cameras focused on the only light pool—Carter—argued that they were paying 80 percent of the cost of Garden lighting, and they wanted light for crowd reaction shots during the acceptance speech. The Carter people won—Convention Manager Andy Shea sided with them, saying he was the landlord of the place.

---

* The longest of the 94 bomb alert conditions during the Convention— one hour—came during Carter's acceptance speech. The alert system consisted of four conditions: Possible Blue—a credible threat has been received or a suspicious object has been found; Blue—a search is under way or the object (a package, for instance) is being inspected; Orange— an object has been inspected and is dangerous, prepare for evacuation; Red—evacuate. In "Red" condition DNC Chairman Strauss would have gone to the podium and announced that the air conditioning had broken down and delegates and guests should leave the hall. Possible Blue and Condition Blue were the only alerts signaled during the Convention.

The only problem with the Carter campaign's plan was that the Garden had no light-dimming system—the things were either on or off. The surges of current while the lights were going up and down might blow the Garden's main circuit-breakers, leaving Carter to accept the nomination by flashlight or candles. The session, scheduled to begin at 1:00 P.M., got under way almost an hour late because network and Garden electricians, working together for a change, were plotting and replotting the building's circuitry. By 5:30, they finally figured that it could be done safely— if the air conditioning was shut down. That was why, out in the Ohio delegation, Clare Smith was so cold—the air conditioning was on full blast, lowering the temperature of the hall to compensate for the heat that was going to build up when Carter came on, the lights dimmed, and the cooling shut off.

It took a half-hour to get the podium ready for the entrance of the nominees, as chairs were set up for the Carter and Mondale families and staffs, and Bob Tisch, the chairman of Loews, hustled back and forth emptying ashtrays and wastebaskets. All the delegates could see was Bob Strauss and Jerry Rafshoon waving their arms at each other in front of the microphones—both men were animated talkers, and what looked like two Rome traffic cops was just Carter's media man explaining to the party chairman what was going to happen with the lights. The crowd amused itself by batting a couple of red, white, and blue beach balls back and forth in the air, a time-killing trick the Convention planners borrowed from rock concerts.

"What's going on? How do we get to the podium?" asked Betty Rainwater, a former Atlanta schoolteacher who had become Carter's assistant press secretary.

"I don't know," said Griff Ellison, another press assistant.

"I've never been to one of these things before." Not many of the Carter people had. When Jim Gammill, the young Convention coordinator, came to New York in May for his first meeting with DNC officials, he had stood outside the door for several moments, finally taking a deep breath and saying to himself: "What the hell? Here comes the Carter campaign."

Mondale came on at 9:50, absorbing five rousing minutes of political adrenalin from the cheering crowd. Bob Strauss was on his knees behind Mondale whispering, then shouting, "Look left! Look left!"—the still photographers' section was to the left of the podium, and the nominee was not giving them a full-face victory wave.

"For well over a century," Mondale declared, "our nation has been divided North against South and South against North. . . . But tonight we stand together. . . . Our days of discontent are over." He went on for 22 minutes, a vigorous recital of the glories and programs of the Democratic party, but getting his best reaction, an animal roar, with Pat Anderson's line about the sins of the opposition: "We have just lived through the greatest political scandal in American history and are now led by a president who pardoned the person who did it."

The networks switched back and forth between the podium and enthusiastic delegates, Strauss's American montage. "That looks pretty good," Carter said in his trailer, and Jerry Rafshoon decided that dimming the lights was not such a great idea after all. He called Al Vecchione, the DNC's television consultant, on the platform and told him to forget the whole thing. The Carter people had a new idea: the lights would stay up, but Carter would enter the hall from the back, the man of the people coming from the people.

Carter was introduced by a film, a 14-minute piece of masterful propaganda delivered free to 35 million Americans by CBS, NBC, and ABC. Rod Goodwin, an associate of Rafshoon's, put together the Lincolnesque story of a determined barefoot boy from the peanut fields of Plains, Georgia, working his way to a presidential nomination. It was strongest where Carter himself was weakest, using humor and celluloid self-mockery—flashes of political cartoon after cartoon satirizing the man's smile, drive, and self-confidence—to make Jimmy Carter a more likable man than he was. Goodwin poked his head into the trailer where the candidate was seeing the film for the first time and said: "Just kidding, Governor. Don't hold the cartoons against me."

Jimmy Carter came into the hall just before 10:30 P.M. Eastern Daylight Time—the exact time had been put in the Convention schedule ten months before, a symbol of Strauss's determination to catch East Coast television audiences before they went to bed and West Coast audiences at 7:30 P.M., after they were home from the freeways. He moved past the Massachusetts, New Jersey, and Utah delegations, touching hands along the way. It was very impressive. In the press section above the Carter march, Richard Cohen, a *Washington Post* columnist who had had trouble finding things to write about all week, watched the film image dissolve into the man and said: "Son-of-a-bitch! It really is a great story."

In the "Honored Guest" section below the NBC anchor-booth, Mrs. Joseph Powell stood up as Carter came into the hall almost directly beneath her. But the man behind her stayed in his seat—it was George McGovern. Unlike McGovern, Mrs. Powell had never been to a Convention before. Until the day before, she had also never been on an airplane.

Mrs. Powell, who was 58, had always told her civics students at the high school where she had taught for 20 years in Vienna, Georgia, that she was going to see one Democratic Convention before she died. Now she was crying. But she was not looking at Jimmy Carter. She was looking at her 32-year-old son, Jody, who had quit his studies for a Ph.D. in political science to become a volunteer driver for State Senator Jimmy Carter when he first ran for governor in 1966.

As Carter made his triumphant way through the cheering Convention, Wallace delegates in the North Carolina section volunteered to give up their seats so that Carter alternates in the Lower Promenade could come down to the floor and hear their man. Mazie Woodruff stopped that: "There are no Carter or Wallace delegates here anymore—we're all Carter delegates now."

Almost. Larry Morris of Alabama, loyal to George Wallace and his own ambitions to the end, was leaving the hall. With his wife, Beverly, he hailed a taxi on Eighth Avenue and headed uptown, preferring dinner at the Four Seasons to unity with Carter. The driver had a transistor radio on the front seat, and the Morrises heard the waves of acclamation rolling through the Garden. It had not been so bad, Morris said—he had checked off more than 50 new Alabama contacts among delegates, alternates, and hangers-on —"We're building." The radio transmitted Carter's first words: "My name is Jimmy Carter, and I'm running for president." *

Morris turned to his wife, grinned, and said: "My name is Larry Morris, and *I'm* running for governor."

---

* The nominee's opening line, a takeoff on "Jimmy Who?" cracks early in the campaign, and a December, 1974, *Atlanta Journal* headline, JIMMY CARTER IS RUNNING FOR WHAT? was suggested by two television humor writers recruited to add some light touches to the acceptance speech. Jack Kaplan and John Barrett, a couple of former Atlanta advertising writers, were brought in from Los Angeles where they wrote scripts and jokes for, among others, Pat Paulsen and Tony Orlando.

"My name is Jimmy Carter, and I'm running for president.

"It's been a long time since I've said those words for the first time. And now, I'm standing here, after seeing our great country, to accept your nomination.

"Nineteen seventy-six will not be a year of politics as usual. It can be a year of inspiration and hope. . . .

"We feel that moral decay has weakened our country, that it's crippled by a lack of goals and values and that our public officials have lost faith in us.

"It's now a time for healing. We want to have faith again."

Faith, hope, and values. Son-of-a-bitch, it was the same story. Jimmy Carter, a southern Baptist who was neither afraid nor ashamed to mix religion with his politics, hit the same themes that had carried him from national obscurity and the wrong part of the country to this moment. His delivery was soft and emotionless, and the language mixed with his visual use of the tiny town of Plains and his peanut fields on television to project the images of a more fundamental, older America. Perhaps he could reach modern media-bombarded, information-glutted Americans in the same way that leaders communicated in societies with nothing more than word-of-mouth networks—Mohandas Gandhi had done that with the most basic symbolism: fasting, sleeping on a mat, walking barefoot, and riding in the crowded, third-class cars of India's dreadful railroads. There may have been even more symbolism in the fact that Carter's final and most serious challenge came from a student of Gandhi, Jerry Brown, who had rejected a governor's mansion to sleep on a mattress in a bare apartment and rode in a Plymouth instead of a Cadillac limousine.

Jimmy Carter was different, but the delegates listening to him were not sure how. In Plains, they said that you

loved Jimmy Carter in 15 minutes, hated him in 6 months
and understood him in 10 years. The Democrats had known
him less than 6 months.

"We want to be proud again. We just want the truth
again.

"It's time for the people to run the government and not
the other way around. . . . Each time that our nation has
made a serious mistake, the American people have been
excluded from the process. The tragedy of Vietnam and
Cambodia, the disgrace of Watergate, and the embarrassment of the CIA revelations could have been avoided if
our government had simply reflected the sound judgment
and good common sense and high moral character of the
American people.

"The poor, the aged, the weak, the afflicted, must be
treated with respect and compassion, and with love."

Truth and love. They were the kinds of words politicians
avoided—at least, sophisticated national politicians did. But
Carter had made his own rules, learning them by reading
books—an occupation most politicians considered time-
wasting—and by serving the Democratic National Committee in 1974. His reading began with Teddy White's *Making
of the President* series, but did not end there. He even read
political novels, particularly *Dark Horse,* a 1972 best-seller
by Fletcher Knebel about an unknown New Jersey highway
commissioner who captivated the country and almost cap-
tured the presidency with an anti-Washington, anti–big shot
campaign, including a promise never to tell a lie. The cen-
terpiece of Carter's early campaigning had been a pledge,
mocked by opponents and journalists, that "I will never
lie to you."

"All my life I've heard promises about tax reform, but it
never quite happened. With your help, we are finally going
to make it happen, *and you can depend on it!*

"It's time for our government leaders to respect the law

no less than the humblest citizen, so that we can end once and for all a double standard of justice. I see no reason why big-shot crooks should go free, and the poor ones go to jail.

"We have an America that in Bob Dylan's phrase is busy being born, not busy dying.

"This is the America we want. This is the America that we will have.

"We will go forward from this Convention with some differences of opinion, perhaps, but nevertheless united in our calm determination to make our country large and driving and generous in spirit once again; ready to embark on great national deeds and once again, as brothers and sisters, our hearts will swell with pride to call ourselves Americans.

"Thank you very much. God bless you."

Bob Strauss bounced up to the microphone and began a long final cheer of unity, his unity, calling name after name and waving Democrats to the podium: "Senator Scoop Jackson . . . Congressman Morris Udall . . . Senator Frank Church . . . Governor Jerry Brown . . . Governor George Wallace . . . Senator Ed Muskie . . . Senator John Glenn . . . Mayor Richard Daley . . . Senator Hubert H. Humphrey . . . Governor Hugh Carey of New York . . . Governor Raul Castro . . . Congresswoman Barbara Jordan of Texas . . . Mayor Abe Beame of New York . . . Mayor Henry Maier of Milwaukee . . . Governor Reubin Askew, you've been called. Where is Reubin Askew, my good friend? . . ."

Sam Donaldson, a loud and enterprising ABC floor correspondent, went up the stairs behind Askew. Donaldson hadn't been introduced, but the sight of Jimmy Carter waving and smiling up there was too much for him—no one was talking to the candidate and Donaldson was the kind of reporter who abhorred auditory vacuums. He fought his way through the grinning politicians, stuck his microphone in Carter's face, and asked, "Well, did you think you had a snowball's chance at first?"

"I thought I'd win, yes."

"You have that cartoon in your den, though?" Donaldson said.

"Well, it's a great cartoon. It was in the Athens, Georgia, newspaper. They don't like me at all in that newspaper, so they drew a cartoon with me walking in the road carrying a Carter-for-president sign and the devil walking into hell with a snowball. And this guy is standing there and said, 'I'm betting on the snowball.' "

The CBS and NBC control rooms were going absolutely crazy. "Where's Bradley?" screamed Don Hewitt, the CBS floor producer. "For Christ's sake, get up there! Get up there!"

Strauss was going on and on—"Mr. Edward Bennett Williams . . . Governor George Busbee of Georgia"— Jim Teague, the hall manager, was standing at the back of the podium wondering how much weight the temporary floor could really hold. He was not anxious to find out, but his boss kept going—"Senator Cranston . . . Have we missed anybody? Mr. Pat Cunningham of New York . . ."

The applause stopped. There were boos for the man who brought the Convention to New York, the indicted chairman who walked the Garden alone. Ed Bradley, CBS's Carter correspondent, had fought his way up to Carter and Donaldson, and finally stuck his microphone toward the nominee. In the CBS control room nothing came out— Bradley's mike was dead. "Grab the podium mike!" Hewitt yelled. "Grab the podium mike." Bradley turned around and reached in front of Strauss to pull the CBS speakers' mike from its socket, but ABC's Donaldson was still in command. "Governor, have you ever had a finer night than this?"

"No, this is the best night, I think, of my life. Perhaps

with the possible exception of that night when I married my wife 30 years ago. But I can't think of anything in my life that's been this gratifying. To walk in, this is the first time I've seen the hall. I've been watching it from a television screen and you don't get that, you don't get the mammoth nature of it . . ."

"Mr. Arthur Krim, Mr. Lou Archer, Mr. Sheldon Cohen, Mrs. Dorothy Bush," Strauss called. "Our wonderful Convention manager, Mr. Andy Shea . . . *And my wife, Helen Strauss* . . . Mrs. Coretta King . . . The wonderful, the very wonderful Carter staff who led it so far, Mr. Hamilton Jordan, Mr. Jerry Rafshoon, Mr. Jody Powell, Mr. Pat Caddell, not to mention Mr. Charles Kirbo . . . And Joe Fitzpatrick of Virginia . . . Senator Joe Biden . . ."

When Strauss stopped, grinning almost ecstatically, Lindy Boggs, the Convention chairperson, came back to the microphone: "It is a distinct honor for me to recognize the Reverend Martin Luther King, Sr., of the Ebenezer Baptist Church, Atlanta, Georgia."

Daddy King began in a startling, rolling black basso:

"I would like very much that we would cease walking, talking, in fact, not a word be uttered, unless that word is uttered to *God.*" And there was silence—if God were black and folks, he sounded like this. "Surely *the Lord* is in this place. Surely *the Lord* sent Jimmy Carter to come on out and bring America back where she belongs.

"I'm willing, you are, too, but as I close in prayer, let me tell you, we must close ranks now. If there's any misunderstanding anywhere, if you haven't got a forgiving heart, *get on your knees.* It's time for prayer.

"As I listened to both our leaders, I took a trip up to *heaven,* and I heard those who sleep, who said so much and did so much, and they simply wanted me to tell you, they're still in business, they just moved upstairs.

"You know, let us not forget, this is our Father's world,

and we're His children. Back of this cosmic world, *God* is there operating every moment, on time, and never too late to sing a promise, never.

"I've been doing this sixty-odd years, I've had my trials, my tribulations, my ups and downs, my losses, but I'm determined I'm not going to let *nothing* get me down.

"I'm going on and see what the end is going to be to all of this.

"The Lord bless *you* and keep *you,* The Lord make His face to shine upon *you,* and be gracious unto *you.* The Lord lift up the light of His countenance upon *you* and give you peace, now and always.

"Amen."

Strauss signaled Peter Duchin, and the orchestra began playing "We Shall Overcome!" Tom Hayden of New York Telephone signaled his men to move onto the floor and get the 220 red-and-white phones in delegations before they became souvenirs. Steve Alper, the unit manager of the television-audio Pool, was already climbing over chairs gathering up the 56 delegation microphones before they went the same way. In the loge sections, alternates were using fingernail clippers to try to loosen the screws holding the sleeves of the state standards to the floor. The letters DEMOCRATIC NATIONAL CONVENTION were ripped from the front of the podium before Secret Service agents could get there to protect them—for Strauss, who wanted them for himself.*

As the hymn that had started small wars between southern whites and blacks swept over the hall, Jimmy Carter

---

* Six telephones and one microphonee were taken, along with over 100 chairs. "Six people somewhere are saying that they have the Ohio phone that nominated Jimmy Carter," Hayden said later, "but that's not true. That phone is in my game room at home."

and Coretta King joined hands and began singing. In the North Carolina delegation, Mazie Woodruff, who had sung the words in tougher times, was crying and singing at the same time. She felt an arm go around her shoulders—C. J. Hyatt, George Wallace's state chairman, hugged her and began singing. He whispered to her: "I remember, too."

Dick Jordan, the Secret Service chief, met his wife for dinner after the session. It was the first time he had seen her since coming to New York six weeks before, and he was a very happy man. The Secret Service had really had to go after only three people in New York. A man outside the Garden on Monday night said the Democrats were wasting their time because he planned to kill President Ford before the election. A drunk in a bar near the hall shouted that Jimmy Carter would never get out of New York alive, then told agents it was just a prediction. And a man tried to crash the Carter staff party at the Americana on Wednesday night, claiming that he was a Treasury agent.

After they had a drink, Mrs. Jordan told her husband there were three things he had to take care of—the air conditioner was broken, so was the swimming pool filter, and their son Rick's van wouldn't start.

The Carter family celebrated in suite 2150 of the Americana. At 1:30 there was a knock on the door and an assistant manager of the hotel stood there holding a tray with three bottles of imported champagne.

"We can't sign for them," said Rosalynn Carter, "that's $33 a bottle."

"No, no. They're compliments of the management, Mrs. Carter."

The Carters each took a glass and began passing the wine around. Jimmy Carter told Stan Tretick, the campaign photographer, to put his cameras away—and then the presidential nominee of the Democratic party toasted his family.

Jerry Brown walked back to the McAlpin along West 33rd Street, smiling when a teenager called out: "We want *you* for president, Jerry!"

"Well, keep it in mothballs," Brown yelled back.

Mazie Woodruff left the celebrating downstairs in the Americana just after 1:30. She did not approve of all the drinking. As she stepped outside onto Seventh Avenue, she saw Martin Luther King, Sr., and Coretta King coming in. She hesitated for a moment and then walked up to them and said, "My name is Mazie Woodruff and I just wanted to tell you how much your benediction tonight meant to me."

"God had a hand in all this," Daddy King said. "Maybe we just ought to follow Him." They talked for a while and Mrs. Woodruff told the Kings about her race for Forsyth County commissioner.

"I'd like to help if I could," King said.*

"I've got to get out of this place," Mary Ault said at the bar of The Bottomless Pit. "It's a sewer; the longer you stay around this world, the more shit you see."

Besides that, it had not been a very profitable sewer that week. "I made $300"—half the usual—"Carter got the nomination and I didn't get to meet Hunter Thompson."

Why not just get out? What do you want to do? She said she wanted to be an airline stewardess—that was what she always said. But three times during Convention Week, a

* Reverend King went to Winston-Salem on August 9, drawing 2,000 people, an astounding crowd for a local election, to a rally for Mazie Woodruff, who went on to win election to the county commission.

friend had set up appointments for Mary Ault at airline offices—and three times she did not show up.

Ron Kovic was mobbed as he was wheeled into the lobby of the New York Hilton. "I'm not an eyesore anymore. I'm a person, I'm a person," he exulted to himself as strangers came up to him, congratulating him, saying they had seen him on television, offering him drinks. A man wearing one of the hotel's "Assistant Manager" plaques came over and shook Kovic's hand.

"Do you want the money for the room for tomorrow?" Kovic said.

"No, no," the hotel man answered. "That's quite all right. Don't worry about *that*. I just wanted to say you were great on television tonight."

Clare Smith's date with Rick Weber had been postponed, but she had collected Theodore White's autograph to go with Hunter Thompson's. She had introduced herself to the writer on the floor, telling him that his work had given her the idea of trying to get to the Convention, and he had known she was the youngest delegate. He even began taking notes, and she thought she might make it in the next *Making of the President*. "Wow!"

But the Convention had been less fun for Teddy White than for Clare Smith. He had been displaced as a CBS Convention commentator by Bill Moyers, Lyndon Johnson's former press secretary, who was 20 years younger—and to add insult to that, the network had offered him an "opportunity" to do commentary from the floor, joining the galloping young correspondents and reporters out there. White declined and his agent approached NBC, but Gordon Manning told him, "I'm afraid our plans are already set."

Clare went back to the Sheraton, joining other Ohio dele-

gates for farewell drinks and kidding Benny Bonanno and
Dave Strand about their "councilman talk"—"My col-
leagues" . . . "My constituents." She saw Dan Troy, the
young councilman from Willowick who had become a television image under Joe Kaselak's sponsorship. Which was
strange, because Troy was not much for nightlife, and it
was 2:00 A.M. at Sally's Bar.

"What are you doing here?" she said to Troy.

"I can't stay in my room," he said. "My roommate's
locked in there with some girl."

She laughed and said, "Who's your roommate?"

"Rick Weber."

Theodore H. White, who seemed to have outlived his usefulness to the networks, was still the spiritual father to at
least one generation of political writers. His first campaign
book, *The Making of the President 1960,* had changed the
way politics was perceived in the country, changed the way
it was written about, and thus changed politics itself. It was
worthwhile to go back into his work to find the right phras-
ing for the unchanging workings of the political mind:
"John F. Kennedy in his fourteen years in politics has had
many servants, many aides, many helpers. As he has out-
grown each level of operation, he has gently stripped off his
earlier helpers and retained only those who could go on with
him effectively to the next level."

In the internal memos of the Carter campaign, that process was referred to, less gently, as "the deadwood problem."
Bill vanden Heuvel, the New York coordinator, was deadwood. Landon Butler, whose title in the campaign was "political director," telephoned Boston on the Convention's
final day to formally ask Gerard Doherty, a friend and former campaign manager of Edward Kennedy's, to take over
the New York campaign for the general election.

Doherty had come to the Americana on Tuesday morning, while Jimmy Carter was with the New Jersey delegation, to meet with Butler, Hamilton Jordan, Pat Caddell, and Tim Kraft, the director of field operations.

"What should we be doing in New York?" Butler asked. What about vanden Heuvel?

Bill would be taken care of but, particularly in New York, the Carter people said they needed someone who was an outsider, who was not building a power base. "Everybody thinks he's running for office himself and we can't have that. He'll still have an office and can get his picture in the papers. It's a little delicate, and we won't announce anything for a while. Jimmy's grateful for what Bill's done and there'll be something for him in Washington."

Also, Isabel Hyde, vanden Heuvel's lovely friend who was a volunteer downstairs in the press room, would be brought onto the national staff. "We need some relief from the dogs around here," Jordan said.

Annie gave up on both Broadway and Park Avenue—two girls she knew had been busted uptown already and got 30 days each—and just began her night in the parade on Delancey Street. She made $120, mainly because a truck driver who pulled his van into a side street gave her $80 for a half-hour.

That was it for her. No more work until the Democrats left town and things got back to normal. Anyway, Friday was her birthday. She would be 23, and she wanted to call her mother, whom she sent $150 a week to take care of her 5- and 6-year-old daughters in Dorchester. Then she was going to get drunk by herself.

Senator Hubert Humphrey came out of the Brasserie on East 53rd Street at 3:00 A.M. and a surprised New Yorker quickly asked for his autograph. Humphrey waved him away, but the man had pulled out a pen and piece of paper and insisted. "Would you please let me through?" Humphrey said, walking past him.

Within eight hours of the closing gavel, interviewers working for Louis Harris Associates would be on many of the streets of America—one of the things they would find out in questioning 1,500 voters for the Harris Poll was how well Robert Strauss had done the job he was hired out to do. Polling was anything but an exact science, but that was probably not as important as the fact that the leaders of the country, politicians, based their decisions again and again on the numbers collected by Harris, the other dominant national pollster, George Gallup, and survey researchers for hire like Pat Caddell.

On that basis, the last two Democratic National Conventions had been exciting disasters. In 1968, pre-Convention polling had shown Hubert Humphrey trailing Republican Richard Nixon by 6 percentage points—post-Convention, Humphrey was behind by 15 points. In 1972, pre-Convention polling had shown George McGovern trailing Nixon by 12 points—post-Convention, McGovern was behind by 23 points. As far as Strauss was concerned, those numbers defined the impact of the last two Democratic Conventions.

In the Harris poll before Strauss's Convention, Jimmy Carter was ahead of President Gerald Ford by 13 percentage points. The polling conducted by Harris between July 16 and 19 gave Carter a phenomenal lead of 39 points.

By 3:30 A.M. two bulldozers were roaming the floor of Madison Square Garden breaking up the wooden floor that had been built over the arena's concrete. Above them, workmen smashed in the windows of the network anchor booths —it was cheaper to destroy the $15,000 pieces of glass than to try to get them out of the building.

Bob Strauss was trying to tell his driver where he had seen a 24-hour delicatessen, one of the glories of New York

City in the small hours. He had spent a couple of hours at a joint party of the New York and Texas delegations at the Rainbow Room in Rockefeller Center, leaving with his wife, their three children, and friends. "It'll just take a couple of minutes," he said as they drove back to the Statler Hilton. "I'm that hungry. I want a tongue sandwich more than anything in the world."

He got it—going into the deli, organizing his troops, and placing the order for everyone. Back on the 17th floor of the Statler Hilton, he distributed the sandwiches and said one of the best goodnights of his life.

"Three and a half years, Helen, and it was all worth it. A hundred million people saw it, my Convention," he said, sitting down. "Let's have that tongue sandwich."

"I only have the Swiss cheese I ordered. Do you want half of that?"

"Helen, I don't like Swiss cheese."

⊠ Appendices

Jimmy Carter won the Democratic nomination for president in 56 separate delegate-selection contests beginning with precinct caucuses in Iowa on January 19, 1976, and ending with primary elections in California, New Jersey, and Ohio on June 8 and the Delaware State Democratic Convention on June 12. After his victory in Ohio pushed the Carter delegate total over 1,200—of the 1,505 needed for nomination—large numbers of delegates who were committed to other candidates or who were uncommitted switched their support to the eventual winner. The following chronology of the Carter nomination lists (with the exception of Delaware) delegate totals by candidates before June 10 and the vote at the Democratic National Convention on July 14.

IOWA

January 19

Democrats attending precinct caucuses gave Carter 28 percent of the vote to 13 percent for Birch Bayh, 10 for Fred Harris, 6 for Morris Udall, 3 for Sargent Shriver, 1 for Henry Jackson. Thirty-seven percent was uncommitted.

Delegate count before June 10: Carter—20; Udall—12; Harris—2; uncommitted—13.

Convention vote: Carter—25; Udall—20; Edmund Brown—1; Edward Kennedy—1.

MISSISSIPPI
January 24

Precinct caucuses gave George Wallace 44 percent of the vote to 14 percent for Carter, 12 for Shriver, 2 for Lloyd Bentsen, 1 for Harris. Twenty-seven percent was uncommitted.

Delegate count before June 10: Wallace—11; Carter—5; Shriver—4; uncommitted—4.

Convention vote: Carter—23; abstaining—1.

MAINE
February 7

Municipal caucuses gave Carter 26 percent of the vote to 4 percent for Harris, 4 for Udall, 1 for Bayh. Sixty-four percent was uncommitted.

Delegate count before June 10: Carter—9; Udall—5; uncommitted—6.

Convention vote: Carter—15; Udall—5.

OKLAHOMA
February 7

Precinct caucuses gave Carter 18 percent of the vote to 17 percent for Harris, 13 for Bentsen, 10 for Wallace. Forty percent was uncommitted.

Delegate count before June 10: Carter—12; Harris—7; uncommitted—18.

Convention vote: Carter—32; Harris—3; Barbara Jordan—1; Udall—1.

ALASKA
February 10

Precinct caucuses gave Jackson 6 percent of the vote to 4 percent for Carter. Ninety percent was uncommitted.

Delegate count before June 10: uncommitted—10.

Convention vote: Carter—10.

MINNESOTA
February 24

Precinct caucuses gave Hubert Humphrey 51 percent of the vote to 4 percent for Harris, 2 for Udall. Forty-two percent was uncommitted.

Delegate count before June 10: Humphrey—48; uncommitted—17.

Convention vote: Carter—37; Ellen McCormack—11; Humphrey—9; Harris—4; Udall—2; Brown—1; Fred Stover—1.

NEW HAMPSHIRE
February 24

Carter won the primary election with 30 percent of the vote to 24 percent for Udall, 16 for Bayh, 11 for Harris, 9 for Shriver, 6 for Humphrey.

Delegate count before June 10: Carter—15; Udall—2.

Convention vote: Carter—15; Udall—2.

SOUTH CAROLINA
February 28

Precinct caucuses gave Wallace 28 percent of the vote to 23 percent for Carter. Forty-eight percent was uncommitted.

Delegate count before June 10: Carter—9; Wallace—8; Frank Church—1; uncommitted—13.

Convention vote: Carter—28; Wallace—2; Brown—1.

MASSACHUSETTS
March 2
Jackson won the primary election with 23 percent of the vote to 18 percent for Udall, 17 for Wallace, 14 for Carter, 8 for Harris, 7 for Shriver, 5 for Bayh, 4 for McCormack, 3 for Milton Shapp.

Delegate count before June 10: Jackson—30; Udall—21; Wallace—21; Carter—16; Shriver—7; Harris—6; Bayh—1; McCormack—1; Shapp—1.

Convention vote: Carter—65; Udall—21; Wallace—11; Harris—2; Jackson—2; McCormack—2; Shapp—1.

VERMONT
March 2
Carter won the advisory primary election with 46 percent of the vote to 31 percent for Shriver, 14 for Harris, 9 for McCormack.

Delegate count before June 10: Carter—3; Udall—3; Brown—2; uncommitted—4.

Convention vote: Carter—5; Udall—4; Brown—3.

WASHINGTON
March 2
Precinct caucuses gave Jackson 79 percent of the vote to 6 percent for Udall; 1 for Carter; 1 for Wallace. Twelve percent was uncommitted.

Delegate count before June 10: Jackson—32; Udall—7; uncommitted—14.

Convention vote: Carter—36; Udall—11; Brown—3; Church—2; Jackson—1.

CANAL ZONE
March 6
A party convention chose six uncommitted delegates to cast three votes.

Delegate count before June 10: Church—3.

Convention vote: Carter—3.

FLORIDA

March 9

Carter won the primary election with 34 percent of the vote to 31 percent for Wallace, 24 for Jackson.

Delegate count before June 10: Carter—34; Wallace—26; Jackson—21.

Convention vote: Carter—70; Wallace—10; Brown—1.

HAWAII

March 9

Precinct caucuses gave Udall 5 percent of the vote and less than 1 percent to several other candidates. Eighty-five percent was uncommitted.

Delegate count before June 10: Jackson—1; Udall—1; uncommitted—15.

Convention vote: Carter—17.

WYOMING

March 14

County conventions gave Udall 39 percent of the vote to 30 percent for Carter, 13 for Jackson, 11 for Harris, 5 for Wallace, 2 for Bayh.

Delegate count before June 10: Brown—1; Carter—1; Udall —1; uncommitted—7.

Convention vote: Carter—8; Brown—1; Udall—1.

ILLINOIS

March 16

Favorite son candidate Adlai Stevenson III and Carter ran ahead in a primary election that allocated delegate votes by congressional districts.

Delegate count before June 10: Stevenson—86; Carter—59; Humphrey—4; Wallace—3; Dan Walker—2; uncommitted— 15.

Convention vote: Carter—164; Brown—2; McCormack—1; Udall—1; Wallace—1.

NORTH CAROLINA
March 23

Carter won the primary election with 54 percent of the vote to 35 percent for Wallace, 4 for Jackson, 2 for Udall.

Delegate count before June 10: Carter—36; Wallace—25.

Convention vote: Carter—56; Wallace—3; abstaining—2.

KANSAS
April 3

County conventions gave Carter 38 percent of the vote to 7 percent for Jackson, 4 for Udall. Forty-eight percent was uncommitted.

Delegate count before June 10: Carter—16; Udall—3; Jackson—1; uncommitted—14.

Convention vote: Carter—32; Udall—2.

VIRGINIA
April 3

County and municipal meetings gave 30 percent of the vote to Carter to 9 percent for Udall, 2 for Wallace. Fifty-eight percent was uncommitted.

Delegate count before June 10; Carter—23; Udall—7; uncommitted—24.

Convention vote: Carter—48; Udall—6.

NEW YORK
April 6

Jackson ran ahead in a primary election that allocated delegate votes by congressional districts.

Delegate count before June 10: Jackson—103; Udall—73; Carter—33; uncommitted—65.

Convention vote: Carter—209½; Udall—56½; Brown—4; Jackson—4.

WISCONSIN
April 6
Carter won the primary election with 37 percent of the vote to 36 percent for Udall, 13 for Wallace, 7 for Jackson.

Delegate count before June 10: Carter—26; Udall—25; Wallace—10; Jackson—6; McCormack—1.

Convention vote: Carter—29; Udall—25; Wallace—10; Jackson—3; McCormack—1.

MISSOURI
April 20
Ward and township meetings gave Carter 14 percent of the vote to 6 percent for Udall, 3 for McCormack, 2 for Humphrey, 2 for Jackson, 2 for Wallace. Sixty-seven percent was uncommitted, but many delegates switched to Carter when his candidacy was endorsed by Senator Thomas Eagleton.

Delegate count before June 10: Carter—39; Udall—3; Jackson—1; McCormack—1; uncommitted—27.

Convention vote: Carter—58; McCormack—7; Udall—4; Brown—2.

ARIZONA
April 24
County meetings gave Udall 71 percent of the vote to 10 percent for Carter, 7 for Wallace, 5 for Jackson, 2 for Church.

Delegate count before June 10: Udall—19; Carter—5; Wallace—1.

Convention vote: Udall—19; Carter—6.

PUERTO RICO
April 24
Electoral district caucuses, which had been disrupted and dis-

puted in February, were reconvened and gave Jackson a majority of the commonwealth's delegates.

Delegate count before June 10: Jackson—15; uncommitted —7.

Convention vote: Carter—22.

VIRGIN ISLANDS
April 24

At mass meetings on St. Thomas and St. Croix three uncommitted delegates were selected.

Delegate count before June 10: uncommitted—3.

Convention vote: Carter—3.

NORTH DAKOTA
April 27

Precinct caucuses gave Humphrey 7 percent of the vote to 3 percent for Carter. Ninety percent was uncommitted.

Delegate count before June 10: uncommitted—13.

Convention vote: Carter—13.

PENNSYLVANIA
April 27

Carter won the primary election with 37 percent of the vote to 25 percent for Jackson, 19 for Udall, 11 for Wallace.

Delegate count before June 10: Carter—66; Udall—23; Jackson—20; Shapp—17; Wallace—3; uncommitted—49.

Convention vote: Carter—151; Udall—21; Brown—6.

NEW MEXICO
April 29

County conventions gave Carter 44 percent of the vote to 28 percent for Udall. Twenty-eight percent was uncommitted.

Delegate count before June 10: Carter—9; Udall—6; uncommitted—3.

Convention vote: Carter—14; Udall—4.

GUAM
May 1

At a party mass meeting, three uncommitted delegates were selected.

Delegate count before June 10: uncommitted—3.

Convention vote: Carter—3.

LOUISIANA
May 1

Carter won 10 delegates in the primary election to 7 delegates for Wallace. Fifteen other delegates were uncommitted. Nine were chosen by the state Democratic Central Committee, in the same proportion as those elected in the primary.

Delegate count before June 10: Carter—13; Wallace—9; uncommitted—19.

Convention vote: Carter—35; Wallace—5; Brown—1.

TEXAS
May 1

Carter won 92 of 98 delegates selected by congressional districts in the primary election, with 32 more selected at a state convention on June 18.

Delegate count before June 10: Carter—112; Bentsen—6; Brown—2; Wallace—1; uncommitted—9.

Convention vote: Carter—124; Brown—4; Leon Jaworski—1; Wallace—1.

COLORADO
May 3

Precinct caucuses gave Carter 23 percent of the vote to 14 percent for Udall, 13 for Church, 7 for Brown.

Delegate count before June 10: Udall—4; Brown—2; Carter—2; Church—2; uncommitted—25.

Convention vote: Carter—15; Brown—11; Udall—6; Church—3.

ALABAMA

May 4

Wallace won the primary election with 51 percent of the vote to 27 percent for Carter.

Delegate count before June 10: Wallace—27; Carter—3; uncommitted—5.

Convention vote: Carter—30; Wallace—5.

DISTRICT OF COLUMBIA

May 4

Carter won the primary election with 40 percent of the vote to 26 percent for Udall.

Delegate count before June 10: Carter—8; Udall—5; uncommitted—4.

Convention vote: Carter—12; Udall—5.

GEORGIA

May 4

Carter won the primary election with 84 percent of the vote to 11 percent for Wallace, 2 for Udall.

Delegate count before June 10: Carter—50.

Convention vote: Carter—50.

INDIANA

May 4

Carter won the primary election with 68 percent of the vote to 15 percent for Wallace, 12 for Jackson, 5 for McCormack.

Delegate count before June 10: Carter—51; Wallace—10; uncommitted—14.

Convention vote: Carter—72; Wallace—3.

CONNECTICUT
May 11

Town primary elections gave Carter 33 percent of the vote to 31 percent for Udall, 18 for Jackson, 5 for McCormack. Thirteen percent was uncommitted.

Delegate count before June 10: Carter—35; Udall—16.

Convention vote: Carter—35; Udall—16.

NEBRASKA
May 11

Church won the primary election with 39 percent of the vote to 38 percent for Carter, 7 for Humphrey.

Delegate count before June 10: Church—15; Carter—8.

Convention vote: Carter—20; Brown—3.

WEST VIRGINIA
May 11

Favorite son Robert Byrd won the primary election with 89 percent of the vote to 11 percent for Wallace.

Delegate count before June 10: uncommitted—33.

Convention vote: Carter—30; Byrd—1; Jennings Randolph —1; Udall—1.

UTAH
May 17

District mass meetings gave Church 23 percent of the vote to 16 percent for Carter. Forty-one percent was uncommitted.

Delegate count before June 10: Church—5; Carter—4; uncommitted—9.

Convention vote: Carter—10; Brown—5; Cesar Chavez—1; Church—1; Shapp—1.

MARYLAND
May 18
Brown won 49 percent of the vote in the advisory primary election to 37 percent for Carter, 5 for Udall, 4 for Wallace. But delegates were chosen from slates entered by congressional districts, and there were no Brown slates.

Delegate count before June 10: Carter—32; Jackson—10; Udall—7; uncommitted—4.

Convention vote: Carter—44; Udall—6; Brown—3.

MICHIGAN
May 18
Carter won the primary election with 44 percent of the vote to 43 percent for Udall, 7 for Wallace.

Delegate count before June 10: Carter—69; Udall—58; Wallace—2; uncommitted—4.

Convention vote: Carter—75; Udall—58.

DEMOCRATS ABROAD
May 24
Mail ballots from Democrats living outside the United States were counted in London.

Delegate count before June 10: Brown—½; uncommitted— 2½.

Convention vote: Carter—2½; Brown—½.

ARKANSAS
May 25
Carter won the primary election with 63 percent of the vote to 16 percent for Wallace, 8 for Udall, 2 for Jackson.

Delegate count before June 10: Carter—17; Wallace—5; Udall—1; uncommitted—3.

Convention vote: Carter—25; Udall—1.

IDAHO
May 25

Church won the primary election with 80 percent of the vote to 12 percent for Carter, 2 for Humphrey.

Delegate count before June 10: Church—14; Carter—2.

Convention vote: Carter—16.

KENTUCKY
May 25

Carter won the primary election with 59 percent of the vote to 17 percent for Wallace, 11 for Udall.

Delegate count before June 10: Carter—37; Wallace—7; Udall—2.

Convention vote: Carter—39; Wallace—5; Udall—2.

OREGON
May 25

Church won the primary election with 34 percent of the vote to 27 percent for Carter and 25 percent for Brown, who ran as a write-in candidate.

Delegate count before June 10: Church—14; Carter—11; Brown—9.

Convention vote: Carter—16; Brown—10; Church—8.

TENNESSEE
May 25

Carter won the primary election with 78 percent of the vote to 11 percent for Wallace, 4 for Udall, 2 for Church.

Delegate count before June 10: Carter—36; Wallace—1; uncommitted—9.

Convention vote: Carter—45; Wallace—1.

MONTANA
June 1
Church won the primary election with 60 percent of the vote to 25 percent for Carter, 6 for Udall.

Delegate count before June 10: Church—11; Carter—4; uncommitted—2.

Convention vote: Carter—11; Church—4; Udall—2.

NEVADA
June 1
Brown won the primary election with 53 percent of the vote to 23 percent for Carter, 9 for Church.

Delegate count before June 10: Brown—6; Carter—3; Church—1; uncommitted—1.

Convention vote: Brown—6½; Carter—3; Church—1; abstaining—½.

RHODE ISLAND
June 1
Carter won 30 percent of the primary election vote to 28 percent for Church. An uncommitted slate for which Brown had campaigned won 32 percent of the vote.

Delegate count before June 10: Carter—7; Church—6; uncommitted—9.

Convention vote: Carter—22.

SOUTH DAKOTA
June 1
Carter won the primary election with 41 percent of the vote to 33 percent for Udall.

Delegate count before June 10: Carter—9; Udall—7; uncommitted—1.

Convention vote: Carter—11; Udall—5; Humphrey—1.

CALIFORNIA
June 10

Brown won the primary election with 59 percent of the vote to 21 percent for Carter, 7 for Church, 5 for Udall.

Delegate count on June 10: Brown—204; Carter—67; Church—7; Udall—2.

Convention vote: Brown—205; Carter—73; Udall—2.

NEW JERSEY
June 10

Carter won the preferential primary election with 59 percent of the vote, but an uncommitted slate pledged to Brown and Humphrey carried most of the state's congressional districts.

Delegate count on June 10: Carter—25; uncommitted—83.

Convention vote: Carter—108.

OHIO
June 10

Carter won the primary election with 52 percent of the vote to 21 percent for Udall, 14 for Church.

Delegate count on June 10: Carter—126; Udall—20; Louis Stokes—6.

Convention vote: Carter—132; Udall—20.

DELAWARE
June 12

Delegates were selected at a state convention.

Delegate count on June 12: Carter—10; uncommitted—2.

Convention vote: Carter—10½; Brown—1½.

B

This is the questionnaire that Jimmy Carter submitted to the seven men he considered naming as his vice-presidential running mate:

1. Have your federal or state tax returns been the subject of any audit or investigation or inquiry at any time? If so, explain.

2. Has a tax lien or other collection procedures ever been instituted against you by federal, state, or local authorities? If so, please give full details.

3. Would you be willing to give me a detailed financial statement listing all assets and liabilities, including all real property, stock, and other evidences of indebtedness together with a full description of all liabilities? When could this be available for me?

4. If selected as the nominee for vice-president, would you be willing to have the financial statement made public?

5. What outside income have you had since being elected to your present position? If any, give sources.

6. Do you have any campaign funds now on hand? If so, explain.

7. Have you accepted contributions in the past concerning which there may be any question as to legality or propriety? If so, explain.

8. Have you ever been sued in any state or federal court? If so, explain. What court or courts?

9. Have you ever been arrested? If so, where?

10. What is the condition of your health?

11. Have you had a physical recently?

12. Who is your physician?

13. Will you ask that the report of your examination be made available to me?

14. Have you ever had psychiatric or similar treatment? If so, explain.

15. Without details, is there or has there been anything in your personal life which you feel, if known, may be of embarrassment in the presidential election this year in the event you should be a candidate?

16. What about any near relative?

17. Will you furnish me with copies of your federal tax returns for the last five years?

Index